Knocking on Every Door

THE AZRIELI SERIES OF HOLOCAUST SURVIVOR MEMOIRS: PREVIOUSLY PUBLISHED TITLES

Knocking on Every Door
Anka Voticky

FIRST EDITION

The Azrieli Foundation
www.azrielifoundation.org

Cover and book design by Mark Goldstein
Endpaper maps by Martin Gilbert
Inside maps by François Blanc

LIBRARY AND ARCHIVES CANADA CATALOGUING IN PUBLICATION

Voticky, Anka, 1913–
    Knocking on every door / Anka Voticky.

(The Azrieli series of Holocaust survivor memoirs; 3)
Includes bibliographical references and index.
ISBN 978-1-897470-20-6

1. Voticky, Anka, 1913–. 2. Holocaust, Jewish (1939–1945) – Czech Republic –
Personal narratives. 3. Jewish children in the Holocaust – Czech Republic –
Biography. 4. Jewish children in the Holocaust – China – Shanghai – Biography.
5. Holocaust survivors – Canada – Biography. 6. Czech Canadians – Biography.
I. Title. II. Series: Azrieli series of Holocaust survivor memoirs; 3

D804.196.V67 2010   940.53'18092   C2010-905143-2

MIX
From responsible sources
FSC   FSC® C004191
www.fsc.org

PRINTED IN CANADA

The Azrieli Series of Holocaust Survivor Memoirs

Contents

Series Preface:
In their own words...

In telling these stories, the writers have liberated themselves. For so many years we did not speak about it, even when we became free people living in a free society. Now, when at last we are writing about what happened to us in this dark period of history, knowing that our stories will be read and live on, it is possible for us to feel truly free. These unique historical documents put a face on what was lost, and allow readers to grasp the enormity of what happened to six million Jews – one story at a time.

David J. Azrieli, C.M., C.Q., M.Arch
Holocaust survivor and founder, The Azrieli Foundation

Since the end of World War II, over 30,000 Jewish Holocaust survivors have immigrated to Canada. Who they are, where they came from, what they experienced and how they built new lives for themselves and their families are important parts of our Canadian heritage. The Azrieli Foundation's Holocaust Survivor Memoirs Program was established to preserve and share the memoirs written by those who survived the twentieth-century Nazi genocide of the Jews of Europe and later made their way to Canada. The program is guided by the conviction that each survivor of the Holocaust has a remarkable story to tell, and that such stories play an important role in education about tolerance and diversity.

Millions of individual stories are lost to us forever. By preserving the stories written by survivors and making them widely available to a broad audience, the Azrieli Series of Holocaust Survivor Memoirs seeks to sustain the memory of all those who perished at the hands of hatred, abetted by indifference and apathy. The personal accounts of those who survived against all odds are as different as the people who wrote them, but all demonstrate the courage, strength, wit and luck that it took to prevail and survive in such terrible adversity. The memoirs are also moving tributes to people – strangers and friends – who risked their lives to help others, and who, through acts of kindness and decency in the darkest of moments, frequently helped the persecuted maintain faith in humanity and courage to endure. These accounts offer inspiration to all, as does the survivors' desire to share their experiences so that new generations can learn from them.

The Holocaust Survivor Memoirs Program collects, archives and publishes these distinctive records and the print editions are available free of charge to libraries, educational institutions and Holocaust-education programs across Canada, and to the general public at Azrieli Foundation educational events. Online editions of the books are available free of charge on our web site, www.azrielifoundation.org.

The Azrieli Foundation would like to express appreciation to the following people for their invaluable efforts in producing this series: Mary Arvanitakis, Josée Bégaud, Florence Buathier, Franklin Carter, Mark Celinscack, Darrel Dickson (Maracle Press), Andrea Geddes Poole, Sir Martin Gilbert, Pascale Goulias-Didiez, Stan Greenspan, Karen Helm, Carson Phillips, Pearl Saban, Jody Spiegel, Erika Tucker, Lise Viens, and Margie Wolfe and Emma Rodgers of Second Story Press.

Introduction

Prague, Shanghai, Montreal – these are the main stations of Anka Voticky's extraordinary life journey. In this wise and brilliantly observed memoir, Anka recounts her experiences as a spunky child and pampered young woman in Central Europe, a stateless refugee in China under Japanese occupation, and a survivor of the Holocaust who made a home for herself and her family in post-war Canada. She has a distinctive style – open, direct and surprisingly witty – and a keen eye for those crucial moments that capture a world of meaning. Several threads connect the far-flung events she describes. Evident on every page is her devotion to others, above all her family. Viewed in contrast to her own fierce loyalty, the betrayals she endures are all the more devastating. Anka's odyssey and the fates of her relatives and friends reveal the global reach of the Holocaust, a process of destruction that marked every Jew everywhere as a target for death and rendered every place in the world either a perilous trap or a possible haven. Another recurring theme in the memoir is memory itself. Anka's phenomenal powers of recall make her account vivid and immediate, a gift for the reader. For Anka herself, however, that remarkable ability to remember brings some unbidden, all-too-real, and intensely painful re-appearances of the past.

Anka Kanturkova was born in 1913 in Brandýs nad Labem, a small town in the Austro-Hungarian Empire, just twenty-five kilometres from Prague. Her father, Max Kanturek, owned a men's clothing store and, as was typical of middle-class households in Central Europe at that time, the family had a maid and a nanny. Anka was especially close to Fanda, the maid, a local Czech woman who lived and worked in the household for fourteen years, and Fanda is a significant presence throughout the book. Many memoirs of the period describe similar bonds between Jewish children and gentile maids or nannies. In Czechoslovakia and Poland, it was often those young Christian women who played key roles in sheltering Jewish children during the Holocaust. In some cases, of course, the opposite occurred, and gentiles who worked in Jewish homes turned against their employers, stealing their property and betraying them to the authorities. Fanda remained loyal to Anka and her family, despite the fact that her own father was suspicious of Jews and even believed the old lie that Jews used the blood of Christian children for ritual purposes.

In hindsight, it seems strange that intimate ties between Jews and gentiles could exist alongside such visceral antisemitism and ignorance, but this situation too was quite typical. By the time Anka was born in 1913, the approximately two million Jews living under Habsburg rule were an integral part of the economy and society of the multi-ethnic Austro-Hungarian Empire: 300,000 Jewish soldiers and tens of thousands of Jewish officers served the imperial cause in World War I. Yet antisemitism in all its forms was widespread: from old-fashioned religious anti-Judaism to political mobilization against Jewish emancipation to modern, secular racism. Pogroms – violent attacks on Jewish life and property – were not uncommon in periods of crisis, notably in the chaos at the end of World War I.

In 1918, Anka's family moved to Prague, a decision she reports was motivated by her parents' desire to get the best education for their children. No doubt that was true, but as is so often the case, individual and family decisions also reflected wider trends. The decades between 1890 and 1918 saw massive migration of Jews from the countryside and small towns into the major cities of Central Europe.

This movement was part of a wider process of urbanization through-out Europe, although Jews were even more likely than non-Jews to participate. Cities provided economic, professional, educational and cultural opportunities; they also offered increased security (strength in numbers) and access to active Jewish communities. What could Brandýs, with its two hundred-odd Jews, offer compared to Prague, one of the great centres of Jewish life in Europe? In 1918, there were tens of thousands of Jews in Prague, including, most famously, Franz Kafka, whose father, like Anka's, worked in textiles. In the follow-ing years, thousands more streamed in from small towns throughout Bohemia, so that by 1939, 20 per cent of the city's population was Jewish.

By the time Anka was six years old, the Austro-Hungarian Empire had dissolved and Prague became the capital of the newly estab-lished Republic of Czechoslovakia. Its founder and first president was Tomáš Garrigue Masaryk, whose birthday, March 7, became a Czechoslovak national holiday. In 1944, Anka notes, the Germans in charge of Auschwitz "celebrated" that date by gassing almost 4,000 Czech Jews, including one of her cousins. Anka's father, like many of his contemporaries, was a staunch Czech patriot who saw no con-tradiction between being Czech and being Jewish. Indeed, ethnic identities and linguistic and religious practices were quite flexible for many citizens of Czechoslovakia until the late 1930s. Anka recalls the Roman Catholic prayers she learned as a little girl and the patriotic poem she recited before the Club of Czech Jewish Women. Czech Jews were involved in all but the most restrictive political parties and even Zionists participated actively in the life of the new democracy and sought ways to make Jews "at home" in Czechoslovakia.

For Anka's family, as for many citizens of Czechoslovakia's first re-public, Czech patriotism did not mean rejection of all things German. To the contrary, knowledge of the German language opened eco-nomic, social and cultural opportunities, and many families, Jewish and Christian, went to considerable effort to ensure that their children were bilingual. Anka's mother was no exception and arranged for Anka and her younger sister, Liza, to learn German, whether they wanted to or not. On numerous occasions as an adult, Anka's fluent German proved decisive in negotiating dangerous situations. German also served as the lingua franca among the Jewish refugees in Shanghai, the vast majority of whom came from Germany and Austria.

A prominent theme throughout Anka Voticky's memoir is the importance of family. To her father, Anka tells us, family was everything and it is clear that she shares that view. Throughout the book she names aunts, uncles, cousins and cousins' cousins, and recounts what she knows of their fates. An aunt and a cousin drowned when their ship sank en route to Palestine. A maternal uncle made it to England with his wife and children; his brother committed suicide in Prague. These and the many other such notices that appear in the memoir are a way to remember and honour the dead and acknowledge the far smaller number of Anka's relatives who survived. They are also the result of hard-won knowledge, bits of information Anka pieced together from diverse sources and patiently assembled over time. Sixty years after the war ended, Anka was still learning what had happened to members of her extended family.

For Anka's family and other Czech Jews, the dream of finding a permanent place in the Czechoslovak republic ended even before World War II began. In 1933, the same year that Anka married her persistent suitor, Arnold Voticky, Adolf Hitler became chancellor of Germany. By 1935, Nazi Germany had introduced conscription and was engaged in a massive program of rearmament, in direct defiance of the post-war settlements that had created the independent countries of Czechoslovakia and Poland. Hitler's vision of Europe included no place for those nations. In a 1937 meeting with leaders of the German army, navy and air force, Hitler announced his plans for a series of wars of conquest, to win "living space" (*Lebensraum*) for the German people. He identified Czechoslovakia as his first target.

Anka was not oblivious to these developments, but she was preoccupied with family matters: her first child was born in 1933, her second in 1937. When Czechs, panicked by German rearmament, rushed to buy gas masks, Anka's main concern was where to find one that fit her two-year-old.

Following Nazi Germany's annexation of Austria in the spring of 1938, Hitler and his followers turned their attention to Czechoslovakia. The issue they used to generate a crisis was the ethnic German minority in the Sudetenland, near the border with Germany. In the summer of 1938, members of the ethnic German population became increasingly vocal with complaints of mistreatment at the hands of the Czech government. Nazi agents encouraged and provoked that discontent. In response to reports that Hitler planned military action to rescue the Sudeten Germans, the Czechs began to mobilize their own forces. They also appealed to the French and the British for help. Alarmed at the risk of war, representatives of the European powers agreed to meet with Czech and German negotiators to seek a resolution. At the Munich Conference in September 1938, French and British delegates decided Czechoslovakia should cede the Sudetenland to Germany.

Decades after the Munich Conference, it and its most famous spokesman, British prime minister Neville Chamberlain, are still synonymous with the term "appeasement." The term is almost always invoked with contempt, and Chamberlain is mocked for his triumphant announcement that he and his colleagues had achieved peace for their time. Perhaps Chamberlain and the others showed weakness, but they wanted peace, whereas Hitler was set on war. Instead of rejoicing at his successful manoeuvre, Hitler considered it a failure to return to Berlin with a negotiated settlement. He regarded Czechoslovakia as an easy target and worried that now Germany's more formidable enemies would have time to prepare for confrontation. It had been a terrible mistake, Hitler later insisted, to have allowed the "Schweinehund" Chamberlain to cheat him out of war in 1938.

Alarmed by events and aware of the suffering of Jews in Germany and annexed Austria, Arnold Voticky began seeking ways to get his family out of the country. Although these early efforts failed, steps he took at this stage proved crucial later and Anka credits her survival largely to her husband's foresight. Meanwhile, the situation only got worse. In March 1939, in violation of the accord signed at Munich, German troops entered the rest of Czechoslovakia. On Hitler's orders the state was dismantled. Parts were incorporated into the German Reich and other territories, including the city of Prague, were set up as the Reich Protectorate of Bohemia and Moravia, a kind of colony of Nazi Germany. Anyone who has ever asked, "Why didn't the Jews leave?" will gain valuable insights from Anka's memoir. Members of her family showed enormous ingenuity and expended considerable time and money in devising plans for escape to the United States, England, Palestine and Yugoslavia. All came to naught. Anka did manage to enter Italy with her two small children, but stranded there with no prospect of reuniting with her husband, parents and sister, she returned to Prague in July 1939. "Only after the war," she writes, "did I fully realize what a terrible decision that was."

Anka Voticky's memoir provides unforgettable proof of the international scope of the Holocaust. Less than 10 per cent of Czech Jews – some 26,000 people – managed to escape the Nazi trap through emigration. Efforts to find refuge and establish homes brought Jews from Anka's circle of acquaintance to every continent. For Anka the trajectory led from Europe to East Asia and finally Canada. Other people she knew followed paths of escape that led out of Europe to Palestine, Africa, India, Latin America, Australia and the United States.

Anka and her family succeeded in reaching a safe haven, but many of the people she describes did not. More than 250,000 Czech Jews were murdered in the Holocaust. The vast majority were sent to Theresienstadt (Terezin); 80 per cent of them were killed in Treblinka, Sobibor, Majdanek and Auschwitz-Birkenau. No doubt many had also tried to escape, had made the rounds of consulates, tried their luck at the border, and pleaded with distant relatives and strangers for help – but the odds against them were horrendous. Transportation routes disappeared under the pressures of war; governments, worried about floods of refugees, shut their borders; exit visas were refused and transit visas expired; funds ran out; officials, go-betweens and sometimes even trusted friends and family members failed to follow through on promises of help, stole from and betrayed refugees made vulnerable by desperation. Anka's memoir reminds us that we have first-hand accounts only from those who survived. Her sensitivity to the many who tried but failed to get out in time contributes to the immense value of her book.

Finally, in April 1940, Anka and a group of ten family members and friends succeeded in leaving Prague en route to what seemed to them an unlikely and unappealing destination: Shanghai. They were not alone. Between 1938 and 1941, almost 20,000 European Jews took refuge in the International Settlement in Shanghai, an area established by the Treaty of Nanking in 1842, at the end of the First Opium War between Britain and China. When the Japanese occupied Shanghai in 1937, they did not institute passport or visa requirements in the International Settlement. As a result, Jewish refugees, including the many who, like Anka and her family, were officially stateless, could enter those parts of the city and even settle there – provided they could reach Shanghai.

It is impossible to overestimate the difficulty of getting from Central Europe to East Asia in the midst of a world war. For European Jews, many of whom had been reduced to destitution under Nazi rule, the barriers were even more formidable. Anka and the family members who travelled with her took a route that was open only to those with access to Italy and adequate resources – sailing away from Europe on an ocean liner. Her parents and sister, Liza, followed a different route to Shanghai, one that remained open longer and was used by more European Jews: travelling by train across Siberia and then via Kobe, Japan. Both options required a welter of exit and transit visas, tickets for transportation, food along the way, and often bribes for uncooperative officials.

In the summer of 1940, Chiune Sugihara, a Japanese diplomat stationed in Kovno/Kaunas, Lithuania – then under Soviet occupation – issued thousands of visas permitting Jewish refugees to transit through Japanese territory. He did so on his own initiative, against the instructions of his superiors. Almost all of the Lithuanian and Polish Jews who arrived in Shanghai did so with Sugihara visas. Among them were over three hundred students and teachers from the Mir Yeshiva in Poland, the only entire seminary for Jewish religious study to survive the Holocaust. Also travelling with Sugihara visas were Anka's sister and her parents. All these opportunities proved fleeting. Over the course of 1941, with the entry into the war of the Soviet Union in June and the United States in December, every passageway into Shanghai slammed shut. Even so, the Chinese port city sheltered more European Jews from the Holocaust than did all the Commonwealth countries put together.

The vast majority of Jews who reached Shanghai were German and Austrian; Jews from Poland and Lithuania were a distinct minority, and Czech Jews are rarely mentioned in scholarly or memoir accounts. Anka's descriptions of life in Shanghai show that she had contacts with refugees from many parts of Europe, including with members of the large Russian colony that had existed in the city since the Russian revolution in 1917. Until 1943, Jews in Shanghai had considerable freedom. That year, under pressure from their German allies, the Japanese issued the Ghetto Proclamation requiring all Central European Jews to live in the Hongkew (Hongkou) district. There Anka and her family remained until the war ended on August 12, 1945.

Two weeks later, the ghetto was officially opened and American military detachments set up shop in the city, accompanied by representatives of the Joint Distribution Committee and the United

Nations Relief and Rehabilitation Administration (UNRRA). Shanghai had protected Anka and her family but it also isolated them from news of relatives and friends who had remained in Europe. Only in September 1945 did she and Arnold learn what had happened to most of the Voticky family.

Most of the Jewish refugees who had come to Shanghai left once the war was over and by the late 1950s, the Jewish "ghetto" had all but vanished. Anka and her family were no exception: in July 1946 they set sail on an American military ship, headed not to the United States but to Europe. It was a natural decision – to go home – and in September they arrived in Prague. Instead of the longed-for comfort and relief, however, they met with bitter disappointment. By mid-1948, just months after the Communists took over Czechoslovakia, the Votickys left again, this time travelling via Belgium, London and New York to Canada.

Anka's post-war "homecoming" was distressing and terrible, and, sadly, it was not unique. Many Jewish survivors who returned to Germany, Austria, Poland, Hungary and elsewhere experienced hostility, even violence. There were incidents in occupied Germany when Germans, including policemen, attacked and beat Jews in Displaced Persons camps, usually on the accusation that young Jewish men were black marketeers and troublemakers. Neighbours who had "taken care" of Jewish property often refused to return it or even to acknowledge its origins; "You're still alive?" was a common greeting to Jews who came back. Polish Christians killed an estimated 2,000 Jews in the two years following the war, more than forty of them in the 1946 pogrom in Kielce. Numbers were lower in Hungary, but there, too, many Jews who returned – to look for family members and friends, to reclaim belongings, to live – were hounded out and hundreds were killed. The single most violent incident in post-war Czechoslovakia was the September 1945 pogrom in Topol'čany, where local Slovaks seriously injured forty-eight Jews. Soon afterward, all of the 550 Jews who had returned to the town left.

Greed explains some of this violence: as Anka shows, gentiles of all kinds had benefited from the "removal" of Jews during the war and they were unlikely to surrender their gains willingly. Antisemitism was an obvious factor too, as were the residual effects of Nazi propaganda. During years of war and devastation, people had grown accustomed to violence and, as Anka notes in her memoir, a general brutalization of life was also evident in the post-war attacks on ethnic Germans in Czechoslovakia. The shame of a bad conscience played a particular role in antisemitic outbursts: people who had abandoned and betrayed Jews, and participated in, witnessed or profited from violence against them, found the presence of Jewish survivors a reproach and feared their revenge.

Yet another influence – official sanction – was at work in areas liberated and occupied by the Soviet Union and, subsequently, under Communist rule. Non-Jews soon learned that attacks on Jews were not only tolerated, but that they sometimes originated at the highest levels of government, starting with Joseph Stalin himself. In Czechoslovakia, the Communist Party came to power by a coup d'état in 1948, just as Stalin's campaign against "rootless cosmopolitans" – a codeword for Jews – was gathering force. Once again, Anka and her husband showed ingenuity and foresight in arranging to leave. Their motives and methods were particular to them, but thousands of other Jews responded the same way. By 1950, half of the 15,000 Czech Jewish survivors in the country had departed for Israel. More followed in the wake of the Slánský affair of 1952. That year Czech Stalinists, with backing from Moscow, accused Rudolf Slánský, the First Secretary of the Communist Party of Czechoslovakia, and thirteen other prominent Communists of high treason. Eleven of the fourteen defendants were Jewish by origin and accusations of a Zionist-led conspiracy against the "people's democracy" of Czechoslovakia were central in the state trial. All fourteen men were found guilty and eleven were sentenced to death. The message could not have been clearer: Jews were officially unwanted.

Anka and Arnold Voticky arrived in Canada on July 1, 1948, with their two children; a third was born in Montreal in 1949. This last and by far longest chapter of Anka's life began with indecision. Originally destined for Toronto, the Votickys changed their minds at the urging of friends from Shanghai and settled in Montreal instead. The challenges they faced were unique to them yet part of wider trends, too. Between 1946 and 1960, some 46,000 Jews immigrated to Canada, a country whose Jewish population prior to the war had been quite small. As a result, by the 1990s, Canada had a higher proportion of Holocaust survivors and their families among its Jewish communities – 30 to 40 per cent – than any other diaspora community.

Like most immigrants, Anka and her family struggled to create a place for themselves in their new country. Their location in Montreal brought opportunities but also particular frustrations and concerns. Financially, times were tough: Arnold found that the jewellery businesses he had successfully built up in Europe and China could not gain a foothold in Canada. By 1950 almost all of their Shanghai friends had moved away, and illnesses and deaths of loved ones meant additional worry and loneliness. Still, Anka made contact with other survivors and with educational projects – through the Holocaust Memorial Centre, which opened in the 1970s, and the Living Testimonies project at McGill University. An amateur photographer, Arnold Voticky had filmed key passages in his family's life with an 8mm camera and his footage was featured in a major documentary, *The Port of Last Resort*, a 1999 Austrian-American co-production.

The political climate in Quebec in the 1990s added further challenges. In 1995, by a tiny margin, the province's voters said no in a referendum on Quebec independence. Then-Parti Québécois leader Jacques Parizeau publicly blamed the outcome on "money and the ethnic vote." Those who heard echoes of antisemitism in that accusation confirmed their suspicions when Pierre Bourgault, another long-time separatist, lashed out against "the Jews, the Italians and the Greeks" as "racists" who "vote in an ethnic bloc." The following year, B'nai Brith and the Canadian Jewish Congress observed anxiety among Quebec Jews around a number of high-profile incidents. One of them, in which Anka Voticky played a part, involved a Radio-Canada reporter named Normand Lester. Claiming that nurses at the Jewish General Hospital in Montreal had refused to provide treatment in French, Lester organized a public protest in front of what is one of the largest and most influential research hospitals in Canada. The Jewish General weathered that storm and fourteen years later made news again when Jacques Parizeau, by then a former premier of Quebec, fell ill and chose to be treated in that very hospital.

Anka Voticky's remarkable memoir spans three continents and almost an entire century. Her memories of the Hitler years, of the destruction of the Jewish communities of Europe and of the war of annihilation that she survived in Shanghai, are the recollections of an adult. She experienced those events as an independent person whose decisions and actions were crucial not only to her own survival but to that of her children and her parents. The down-to-earth advice with which she closes her book adds an important message to the often-quoted warning of the philosopher George Santayana: "Those who cannot remember the past are condemned to repeat it." Those who do remember and indeed cannot forget the past, Anka Voticky shows – those who with open eyes and hearts truly see and feel the past in the present – have something valuable to teach us about how to live in the world.

Doris Bergen
University of Toronto
2010

LIST OF SOURCES AND SUGGESTIONS FOR FURTHER READING:

Bergen, Doris L. *The Holocaust: A Concise History*. Lanham, MD: Rowman and Littlefield, 2009.

Bluman, Barbara Ruth. *I Have My Mother's Eyes: A Holocaust Memoir Across Generations*. Vancouver, BC: Ronsdale Press, 2009.

Bryant, Chad. *Prague in Black: Nazi Rule and Czech Nationalism*. Cambridge, MA: Harvard University Press, 2007.

Dwork, Debórah and Robert Jan Van Pelt. *Flight from the Reich: Refugee Jews, 1933–1946*. New York: W.W. Norton, 2009.

Falbaum, Berl, ed. *Shanghai Remembered: Stories from Jews Who Escaped to Shanghai from Nazi Europe*. Royal Oak, MI: Momentum Books, 2005.

Friedländer, Saul. *Nazi Germany and the Jews, 1933–1945*. Abridged by Orna Kenan. New York: HarperCollins, 2009.

Kovály, Heda. *Under a Cruel Star: A Life in Prague, 1941–1968*. Trans. Franci Epstein and Helen Epstein. New York: Holmes and Meier, 1997.

Kranzler, David. *Japanese, Nazis, and Jews: The Jewish Refugee Community of Shanghai, 1938–1945*. New York: Yeshiva University Press, 1976.

Lichtenstein, Tatjana. "'Making' Jews at home: Zionism and the construction of Jewish nationality in Inter-war Czechoslovakia." *East European Jewish Affairs* 36, no. 1 (June 2006): 49–71.

Port of Last Resort: Zuflucht in Shanghai. (Film) Directed and produced by Joan Grossman and Paul Rosdy, 1998.

Quack, Sybille, ed. *Between Sorrow and Strength: Women Refugees of the Nazi Period*. New York: Cambridge University Press, 1995.

Rothkirchen, Livia. *The Jews of Bohemia and Moravia: Facing the Holocaust*. Lincoln, NE: University of Nebraska Press, 2005.

Rozenblit, Marsha L. *Reconstructing a National Identity: The Jews of Habsburg Austria during World War I*. New York: Oxford University Press, 2001.

Weinberg, Gerhard. *A World at Arms: A Global History of World War II*, 2nd edition. New York: Cambridge University Press, 2005.

Zahra, Tara. *Kidnapped Souls: National Indifference and the Battle for Children in the Bohemian Lands, 1900–1948*. Ithaca, NY: Cornell University Press, 2008.

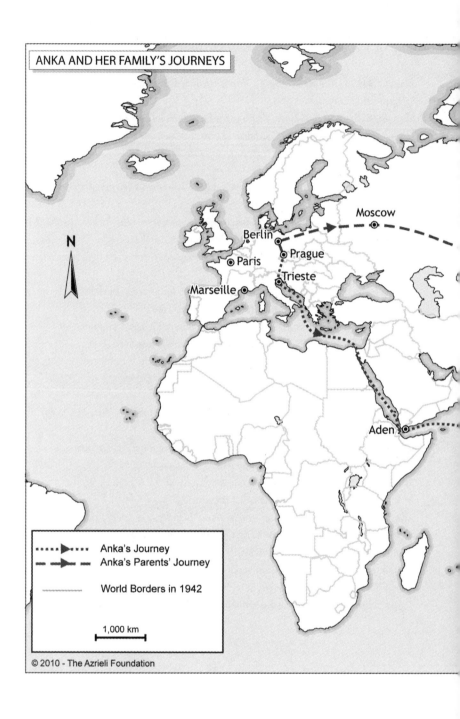

ANKA AND HER FAMILY'S JOURNEYS

N

Moscow

Berlin
Paris
Prague
Trieste
Marseille

Aden

······▶······ Anka's Journey
— — ▶ — — Anka's Parents' Journey

World Borders in 1942

1,000 km

© 2010 - The Azrieli Foundation

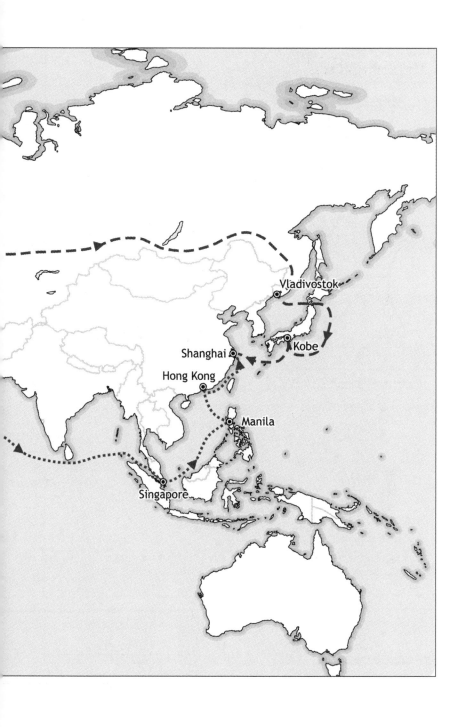

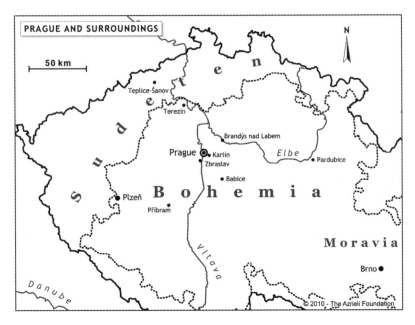

PRAGUE AND SURROUNDINGS

50 km

N

S u d e t e n

Teplice-Šanov

Terezín

Brandýs nad Labem

Elbe

Prague · Karlín
Zbraslav
Pardubice

· Babice

Plzeň

B o h e m i a

Příbram

Vltava

M o r a v i a

Brno ●

Danube

© 2010 - The Azrieli Foundation

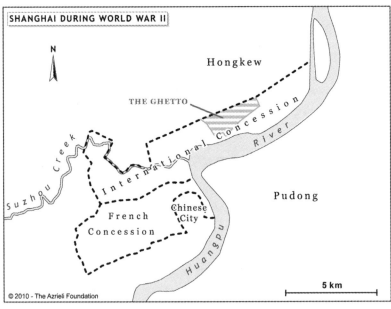

SHANGHAI DURING WORLD WAR II

N

Hongkew

THE GHETTO

I n t e r n a t i o n a l   C o n c e s s i o n

River

S u z h o u   C r e e k

Pudong

French

Chinese
City

Concession

Huangpu

5 km

© 2010 - The Azrieli Foundation

To my husband, Arnold.

They say memories are golden.
Well, maybe that is true.
I never wanted memories.
I only wanted you.

Anka's paternal grandparents: Karel and Charlotte Kanturek

Anka's maternal grandparents: Elizabeth and Abraham Kohn

  – Anka's father: Max Kanturek

  – Anka's mother: Hedvika Kanturek (née Kohn)

    – Anka's eldest brother: Vilda (born 1907)

    – Anka's brother: Erna (born 1908) *married* Hilda (née Müller)

      → *children* (Anka's nieces): Eva, Jana and Carol

  *Anka Voticky (née Kanturek; born 1913)

    married Arnold Voticky

      → *children:* (Anka's son) Milan *married* Cathy

        → *Anka's granddaughters:* Linda & Liza

      (Anka's daughter) Vera *married* Jack Rubin

        → *Anka's grandsons:* Howard and Neil

      (Anka's son) Michael *married* Nancy

        → *Anka's granddaughters:* Allison,
        Candy, Gilly and Ashley

    – Anka's sister: Liza (born 1917) *married* Franta Vilim

      → *children* (Anka's nieces and nephew) Helena, Kathy
      (Kaca) and Tomasek (Tomy)

– Anka's uncle (Max Kanturek's brother): Erwin *married* Malvina

   → *3 children*

– Anka's aunt (Max Kanturek's sister): Heda *married* Siegfried

   → *daughter* (Anka's cousin): Herta

      → *Heda's granddaughter:* Ruth

– Anka's aunt (Hedvika Kanturek's sister): Malva *married* Adolph Gross

   → *children* (Anka's cousins): Karel and Franta

– Anka's aunt (Hedvika Kanturek's sister): Marta *married* Richard Polack

   → *children* (Anka's cousins): Slavek and Jirka

– Anka's uncle (Hedvika Kanturek's brother): Richard *married* Lonca

   → *children* (Anka's cousins): Honza and Hanicka

– Anka's uncle (Hedvika Kanturek's brother): Otto

   → *children* (Anka's cousins): Zdenka and Irma

– Anka's uncle (Hedvika Kanturek's brother): Zigmund *married* Irma

   → *children* (Anka's cousins): Franta and Edith

– Anka's uncle (Hedvika Kanturek's brother): Hugo *married* Kate

   → *children* (Anka's cousins): Leo and Erik

– Anka's uncle (Hedvika Kanturek's brother): Ludvik *married* Hermina

   → *children* (Anka's cousins): Karel and Jirka

– Anka's uncle (Hedvika Kanturek's brother): Emil

A Happy Beginning

I, Anka Voticky, mother, grandmother and great-grandmother, was born Annamarie Kanturek on July 5, 1913, in the town of Brandýs nad Labem, about twenty-five kilometres northeast of Prague. At the time, Brandýs was a part of the Austro-Hungarian Empire, but after the end of World War I, it became part of the new country of Czechoslovakia. The members of my family all became Czech patriots, particularly my father.

I don't remember much about Brandýs from those days – my first memory is from about 1917. After the old Austro-Hungarian emperor Franz Josef died in 1916, the new one, Charles I, passed through our hometown on his coronation tour of Bohemia. What a historic event! My father, who owned a men's clothing store in Peace Square near the centre of the city, had a makeshift platform put up in front of the store for us so that we could see over the crowd. I have hazy memories of our whole family standing on that platform while I, barely four years old, waved a flag.

My father, Max Kanturek, was also born in Brandýs and my mother, Hedvika Kanturek-Kohn, was born in the mining city of Příbram, about ninety kilometres southwest of Brandýs. They were married on June 3, 1906, in the Karlín district of Prague, just east of the city centre. More than twenty-five years later, both my husband, Arnold, and I, and my brother, Erna, and his wife, Hilda, would all be married by the same rabbi, Dr. Hirsch, with the same cantor, Cantor Klein, in the same synagogue.

I was one of four children in our family – my eldest brother, Vilda, was born on June 2, 1907; my brother Erna (Arnost) was born on August 19, 1908; and my younger sister, Liza, was born on February 1, 1917. We were all born in Brandýs.

We had lots of relatives in Prague, Příbram and Pardubice, which is one hundred kilometres east of Prague, but only one grandfather – my mother's father, Abraham Kohn, who lived in Karlín. Our other grandparents had all passed away in 1916, a year of many funerals. That year we buried my father's father, Karel Kanturek, and his wife, Charlotte, as well as Elizabeth Kohn, my mother's mother. I don't remember them since I was only three years old when they died. As a result, I never had a grandmother.

We had to pay regular visits to my grandfather in Prague. He had his own apartment and a housekeeper who kept his house tidy and cooked his meals. We had to present ourselves there on Wednesday afternoons and kiss his hand and I had to make a curtsy – just as if we were visiting a king. That was the traditional, old-fashioned way of showing respect. These visits lasted only about half an hour to an hour.

Although we weren't that close to my grandfather, we were very close to my mother's sisters, Malva and Marta. My maternal grandmother had had eighteen children, but only nine, including my mother, were still alive when I was born – my mother had two sisters and six brothers. My aunt Malva lived in Pardubice, although she came to Prague regularly, and Aunt Marta lived with her husband, Richard Polak, and their two children, Slavek and Jirka, in Příbram. I used to visit their house often – Slavek and Jirka were my age and were like brothers to me. Four of my mother's brothers still lived in Czechoslovakia – Richard, Hugo, Otto and Ludvik. My uncle Zigmund, who passed away in 1916, had moved to Vienna and my uncle Emil had immigrated to the United States.

There were lots of cousins and lots of birthdays in our extended family. I especially remember going to a party for my cousin Hanicka Kohnova, Uncle Richard's daughter. I was never very close to Uncle Hugo's sons Leo and Erik, even though they were my age. Uncle Otto had two daughters, Zdenka and Irma. Uncle Ludvik got married late in life to Hermina Poprova from Libušín, an area that was well known for the huge flocks of geese kept on the local estates. Their two sons, Karel and Jirka, were much younger than I was.

My father only had one brother, Erwin, and one sister, Teta (Aunt) Heda, whom we saw at least once a week. She had a daughter named Herta.

My family moved from Brandýs to Prague, where my father opened another men's clothing store on Maiselova Street in 1918. The main reason for the move was that my parents wanted the best possible education for their children and they assumed that the best schools of higher learning would be in Prague. My eldest brother, Vilda, had just finished elementary school and was about to enter the gymnasium (high school). Our maid, Fanda, who had been a part of our household since 1908 – years before I was born – came with us from Brandýs. Mother later told me a story about Fanda's first year with the family. Just before Passover, Fanda had abruptly left my parents' house to stay with her family for a week.[1] When she came back, my mother asked her why she had gone. After some hesitation, Fanda finally admitted that her father had told her that at Passover, the Jews made matzah with the blood of Christian children.[2] My mother lost

---

1 Passover is a Jewish holiday that takes place over eight days in the spring and commemorates the liberation and exodus of the Israelite slaves from Egypt. For more information, see the glossary.

2 The superstition that Jews used the blood of Christian children during Passover is called the "blood libel"; it is one of the most persistent forms of antisemitism in Europe, dating back to the thirteenth century. Matzah is a crisp unleavened flatbread traditionally eaten during Passover. For more information, see the glossary.

no time in explaining to her what a nonsensical and cruel superstition that was.

Fanda remained with our household until she got married. She was with us for fourteen years and was a second mother to me. Every morning, as soon as I woke up, I would cuddle up in Fanda's bed. She taught me all kinds of things, including Catholic prayers. I remember some of them to this day. I kept in touch with Fanda as much as possible through the turbulent years of my life until her death – and I still remember her fondly. In addition to Fanda, we also had a *Kinderfräulein* – in English she would be called a nanny or governess. She spoke to us in German because it continued to be the primary language of business throughout much of Central Europe and my parents wanted their children to be bilingual.

Our first apartment in Prague was on 11 Rybná Street and we lived in that rented apartment for one year. During that time, almost the whole family got a very bad flu. This was during the worldwide influenza epidemic of 1918. It was a horrible event; millions of people around the world perished. My father was the only one in our family who didn't get sick, so he had to take care of all of us.

I started school while we lived on Rybná Street. I always had a good voice and good diction and I remember my mother asking Mrs. Pelunkova, my Grade 1 teacher, to give me a poem to recite for the Club of Czech Jewish Women. It was a sad poem about an orphaned child – perhaps it was a little sombre for a six-year-old – but my performance was a great success. I can still recite it all from memory. While I was in Grade 1 in that school in downtown Prague, I met two girls who would become my lifelong friends, Lidka Smolkova and Marta Mautnerova.

After our first year in Prague, my family moved again, this time to a building that my father had bought in the Karlín district of the city. The property was actually a complex of two buildings that housed twenty-eight tenants with many children, all of whom became our friends. We were the only Jewish family in the buildings, but I don't remember encountering any antisemitism from the tenants. My father had a partner in this enterprise – our uncle Otto, my mother's brother. I lived in that part of Prague until I got married.

We had a happy childhood and were a very close-knit family. Our parents never went on vacations by themselves. They never even went to movies by themselves – they always took us everywhere. On Sundays they would take me and my sister to Stromovka, an enormous park with a nice restaurant in the centre. There, as a special treat, we would get hot chocolate. We never drank coffee when we were children, but we needed some refreshment – it was a long walk across the city from Karlín. We would occasionally take a streetcar, but often we walked.

In the winter we all skated, skied and tobogganed. When I was six years old I was enrolled in ballet, but at ten, when I was getting really good at it, my mother took me out and sent me for gymnastics instead because she was afraid I would want to become a ballerina. There was always music in our home. My brother Vilda played violin, I took piano lessons and my other brother, Erna, played the zither, a stringed instrument that was fashionable at the time. My mother wanted my sister to also play the piano, but she had no ear for music – she had other talents.

When I was in Grade 3 – I was about nine years old – something momentous happened. I came home from school for lunch and found our apartment full of people. There was a long, festive table, as if we were having a party. I had no idea what was going on until somebody told me that it was Fanda's wedding, and that she would be leaving us. It was a terrible shock; I cried and cried.

Fanda and her husband, Mr. Nebesky, went back to live in Brandýs, where they were both born. I missed her so much that my mother sent me to stay with her for my summer vacation that year. My little sister, Liza, went with me and we all had a good time. We stayed until near the end of August and then went back to Prague to start school on September 1.

I have one very uncomfortable and unforgettable memory of that holiday. I was walking alone across the town square one day when I noticed a blind man playing the violin. On the sidewalk in front of him was his shabby hat, evidently put there to collect donations. The hat was empty – people were just passing by without giving him anything. I felt sorry for him and promptly decided to help by asking him to play a particular piece of music. I can still remember the tune – it was a popular song about bubbles and rainbows. He played it and I danced. I was, after all, taking dance lessons. The passersby now started taking notice and stopped to watch. After the performance I passed the hat. Just as I was presenting the money to the blind man, however, a man came running across the square. Breathless, he asked me, "Aren't you Max Kanturek's daughter?" When I answered that I was indeed his daughter, the man looked shocked. "You just wait!" he told me. "Max is my friend and I am going to write to him right now! He should know what his daughter is doing on the main square of Brandýs – begging!" That really scared me! All I was trying to do was help.

That summer went by quickly and all too soon it came to an end. The grains were harvested and there were Thanksgiving celebrations with music all over the fertile Elbe River region. At the Brandýs Thanksgiving festival someone who knew that I had taken dance lessons asked Fanda if she would allow me to dance. She reluctantly agreed.

It was even better than the performance with the blind man. I now had a whole band behind me! I told the musicians what to play while I danced. After, when I came back to the table, there were bottles of lemonade and platters of cakes and the waiter kept coming by to ask whether there was something he could bring us. I was famous! Soon another man came to our table to talk to Fanda. He told her that there would be a similar celebration in their village the following week – would Fanda let me dance there too? But this time Fanda stood firm. "Once is enough," she said. "She isn't a professional!" That was the end of my dance career.

~

Our mother tongue was Czech, but it was very important to my mother that we all learn proper German, the main language of business in Central Europe. I was obedient, but Liza rebelled – whenever our nanny reminded her to speak German, Liza would start to sing the Czech national anthem. The summer I turned twelve, I spent July and August learning German in a small boarding school in Teplitz-Shönau (in Czech, Teplice-Šanov), a small resort town in northern Bohemia, about ninety kilometres from Prague. The owner was a short, stout lady named Madam Altschule and her school had the same name. While we were there we spoke only German and some of the other students were German girls. We had a really good time. We took swimming lessons and every Saturday we would go to the theatre. As a rule, the plays were German musicals. On Sundays, Mr. and Mrs. Bischicky, good friends of my parents who were originally from Brandýs, would invite me over for the big midday meal.

When I was fifteen, my parents sent me to a large German boarding school in Prachatice in the mountains of the southern Bohemian forest, which is the natural border between Czechoslovakia, Germany and Austria. There were some older girls among the students because the school also had a home-economics college attached to it. At this school, I had to study very seriously to keep up.

As my sister, brothers and I all got older we remained close as a family and continued to have wonderful family outings and events. There was a big fair in Karlín every summer, with swings shaped like small boats, a merry-go-round, and various attractions, contests, circuses and wrestling. We all enjoyed the wrestling, which took place in an especially large tent. My father would buy tickets to the Saturday night wrestling matches and a bag of peanuts for each one of us. My parents also rented a house in the country every summer, somewhere near the water where we could swim. I remember going to the Zbraslav district of Prague on the Vltava River, but there were also other places outside the city – we spent every summer in a different place.

We all still enjoyed music, especially my brother Vilda. There were stacks of classical records and our record player was running all the time. There were the Italian tenors Enrico Caruso and Benjamin Gigli, the violin virtuoso and composer Niccolò Paganini and others. Jazz was becoming very popular by then, but I never acquired a taste for it. For my father's birthdays, we would usually present a family concert. He didn't play any instrument, but before he had gotten married he often went to plays, operas and concerts. Later, he would tell us about the performances he had seen when he was young. And we would talk! After supper, nobody got up right away – we all sat around the table for hours and talked about what had happened during the day.

~

In the summer of 1929, I had just turned sixteen and was enrolled in business school for the fall. After one of my usual Sunday walks with my parents and Liza to Stromovka Park, I met Arnold, my future husband, for the first time – he was twenty. We ran into my brother Erna just outside our house with a young man and twin girls. They were on their way to see a movie, but before they left, Erna asked my mother to give them a snack. We prepared something and set the table. The young man spoke to me, but only a few polite words.

When I woke up the next day, the maid warned me that there was trouble brewing. Apparently Erna had told my parents that his friend liked me – that he thought I was beautiful. That really alarmed my mother because she thought I was much too young to have admirers. She promptly ordered that nobody tell me anything about this. My brother obeyed, but I had nevertheless found out about it from our maid.

That summer, my parents sent me to Italy, to Lido-Alberoni, an island resort spa near Venice. I was with a group of girls from a Jewish community in Brno, in southeastern Czechoslovakia, and I was the only one from Prague. We were all about the same age, ranging from fourteen to sixteen years old, and had a really good time. We met a nice young Italian boy, Francesco Silivri, from Padua, who taught me Italian songs – I still sing them sometimes. We kept in touch for a while after I left, but his letters were in Italian and all I could manage to send were postcards with the words "Multo salute!" (Best Wishes!) Our friendship couldn't last long under those circumstances.

When I returned to Prague by train, my whole family was on the platform waiting for me. Lo and behold, this receiving line included none other than Arnold. I kissed all of my relatives – and Arnold maintained later that I kissed him too. As we were leaving the station, he insinuated himself close enough to me to whisper that he wanted me to meet him on the *korso* – a promenade that took place every Sunday on Prikopy Boulevard. His request shocked me and I refused. I was barely sixteen years old and had never had a date!

Arnold didn't stop calling, however. He would call me on the telephone every day and we'd talk for a half-hour at a time. I still remember our phone numbers to this day – mine was 223–73 and Arnold's was 635–75. He kept asking me to meet him and I kept saying no, but in the end, on Sunday morning, August 13, at eleven, I was on Prikopy Boulevard. Alas, our meeting was ill-fated. Vilda was on a streetcar that was passing by and saw us walking together – what a terrible transgression! By the time I got home, the whole house was in an uproar. My parents had already decided what they were going to do with me: "You are going to Pardubice, to stay with my sister," my mother announced. "You are not going to stay in Prague. This has to stop – you are much too young!"

They called Arnold to come to the house and they put us through a real interrogation, with him in one room and me in another. When my father sat me on his lap, I saw that he was crying. He said that Arnold would "spoil" me and then drop me…. Under such intense pressure, I finally agreed to write Arnold a note saying that we should stop seeing each other. I slid the note under the door between the salon, where I was, and the sitting room where the discussion with him was in progress. That was supposed to be the end of our beautiful romance.

My parents packed me off to Pardubice right away. Mother took me to the station, where I boarded the train and settled myself in the compartment as the train began to move. Confident that the problem was settled, my mother waved goodbye. Before the train could even leave the station, however, the door of my compartment opened and there stood Arnold. In a panic, I asked him what on earth he was doing there. He assured me that he would leave at the next stop, but he had some instructions for me: "Every day after lunch, between twelve and one, your aunt will take a nap like all the mothers do. Go to the post office and there will be a poste restante (general delivery) letter from me. Then call me collect from the post office." Arnold worked at his father's banking house and was a member of the stock exchange – they all took lunch at about a quarter to one. "I'm not going to lose you!" he concluded. I did what he asked.

My brother Erna came to visit me three or four weeks after I had left for Pardubice and stayed for two days. I suspected that he had come to check up on me and I was right – after Erna had left, Arnold told me that my sister, Liza, had told him that Erna had searched under my bed and had found some letters from him in my suitcase. Since we were obviously still communicating with each other, my parents decided that I might as well come home. I returned to Prague and as soon as I walked into my father's store, he greeted me by saying ironically, "Oh, here comes the bride."

Once I was back in Prague, Arnold and I didn't have to meet secretly anymore. I had started business school and Arnold met me after class every day and walked me home. My parents would even invite him to stay for supper. Somehow, we always had a lot to talk about and as soon as Arnold had left my house and gone home, he would head straight to the telephone and call me. Neither of our families could understand it. We had talked all the way from school, had dinner together and then, after all that, we still had to talk to each other on the telephone for another half hour?

During supper one day, my brother Erna told me that I had gotten a call from the Czech Jewish Theatre Club inviting me to come for an audition. It was the beginning of a new season and they were putting on another play. Arnold was surprised and asked what this was about. I told him that my mother was a member of this Jewish community theatre group and every year I took part in their production. They met every Monday in the Urban Café and I had been performing with them since I was six years old. In those days, however, aspiring to be an actress wasn't considered appropriate for middle-class young women and Arnold didn't approve. Before he left that evening, he said to me, "You have to make a decision – it's either theatre or me!" I made the decision not to perform and never regretted it. That was the end of my second artistic career, but I never stopped loving the theatre.

Years later I was given a book written in Czech by a woman who was a member of the same amateur theatre group. In one particular play – my very last performance – she had the role of a princess and I was the prince. The world is a small place indeed. Her maiden name was Hanicka Beckova, but the book was published under her married name, Pravdova. I knew that she had lost her first husband in Auschwitz and I didn't know the name of her second husband, but I recognized her story. I also found a reference to her cousin, Milan Platovsky, who had been another one of the actors in the group. The friend who gave me the book, Jindra, managed to get Hanicka's telephone number in England through the publisher and I got in touch with her.

After the war, when we were visiting Arnold's brother Egon in Santiago, Chile, I met Hanicka's cousin, Milan Platovsky, in a gathering of people who had lived in the Prague community. To introduce myself, instead of saying my name, I recited a few lines from my role as the prince: "Odpust mocný králi že se osmeluji tak záhy zrána předstoupiti před tvou milost." (Forgive me, O powerful king, for having the audacity to ask for your kindness so early in the morning.) From those few words, after all those years, Milan recognized me immediately and called out in surprise, "This is Anka Kanturkova!"[3] I had introduced myself to Hanicka the same way on the telephone.

~

I may have had to stop doing theatre because my boyfriend didn't like it, but in every other respect we really understood each other. Little by little, I got to know his parents as well. One day, when Arnold and I were passing by their house, we saw his mother at the window. This was a popular pastime – people liked to sit with their elbows resting on a pillow on the windowsill and watch what was going on outside. Arnold's mother called out to me, "Miss! Miss! Come in!" but I answered, "Excuse me, gracious lady, I cannot come to your house, my mother wouldn't allow it." Arnold's mother recounted that story to everyone for years. When I went to Italy for the second time, Arnold also went to Lido with his parents. The Votickys stayed in a hotel in Lido while I was with my group in Alberoni, at the end of the island, and they often came to visit me.

It was customary at that time for young people from well-to-do families to take a course in ballroom dancing and deportment in preparation for their introduction to society. Because I had turned sixteen in July, the usual age at which girls took this course, I was registered for it in October. Erna and Arnold also took it (because of me). That winter, my mother had new evening dresses made for me – a different one for each night of the week. At every gathering, though, Arnold insisted on dancing every dance with me – whenever someone else asked me to dance, he promptly cut in. My mother didn't like it at all and begged him to please let me dance with other boys. After all, she explained, this was my debut to society. Arnold,

---

3   In Czech, surnames are modified to reflect one's gender with "ova" added for the feminine form. Anka's father's surname was Kanturek, but the feminine form for Anka's last name was Kanturkova.

however, wasn't taking any chances. He respected my mother, but on this point he was firm – so we danced and danced. He was the kindest, nicest man on earth.

When I finished my courses at the business college I decided to look for work. Arnold was very much against it. He argued that his sister had never worked – it just wasn't done in well-established middle-class families. Still, I wanted to use my new qualifications, so I found myself a job as a bilingual secretary in the office of the Koh-I-Noor pencil manufacturing company. At noon on my first day, I went for lunch and two young men from the office joined me. According to the bon-ton, the custom in polite society, they walked on each side of me. All of a sudden, I noticed Arnold standing nearby. When we got to the restaurant, he took me aside and as soon as we were out of earshot, he announced that I had to have lunch with him – and that I had to quit my job.

Arnold was so insistent that I did quit, but within a week I had found myself another job as a bilingual secretary – this time for an engineer. I hadn't been there very long before the boss told me that he needed me to stay late to take some dictation. I agreed and the boss offered me supper, but I declined. I was quietly working at my desk when, sometime after six o'clock, after everyone else in the building had left, I heard the sound of footsteps in the corridor. Somebody was walking back and forth, back and forth…. The boss heard it too. He opened the door and – there was Arnold! Disgusted, the boss sent me home – and that was the end of yet another promising career.

I still wanted to work, so Arnold gave me a job in his family's banking house. Apparently it was all right for me to work there, but only half a day – the thought of me working all day was too much for Arnold because he thought that I would get overworked. God forbid!

~

Arnold and I got engaged on May 8, 1932. We had a big party to celebrate and then began the preparations for our wedding. We got married a year later, on April 23, 1933, in Karlín. There was a huge reception after the ceremony – I had lots of cousins and not one of them wanted to miss it. After the party, we checked into a hotel near the railway station because our train was leaving early the next morning. We had planned a honeymoon in Austria – we would be spending the first few days in Vienna and the rest of the time in the Alpine village of Semmering.

Alas, we didn't get much sleep that night. There was a telephone in our hotel room and my dear cousins Jirka and Slavek Polak, along with Karel Gross and his brother Franta, called us at regular intervals. They had all had fun at our wedding and, for them, keeping us awake was a lighthearted ending to a beautiful, memorable day.

When we returned from our honeymoon, we had an apartment waiting for us in the centre of town on 11 Josefovská Street. The next morning, my husband went to the office at the bank and then to the stock market. From there, he called to tell me that a business friend of his was in Prague from Vienna and would be having lunch with us.

In Europe, lunch is the main meal of the day. I planned a menu and went shopping like a proper homemaker – we would have chicken soup to start, roasted chicken as a main dish and apple strudel for dessert. Maybe it was overly ambitious of me – this would be the first strudel I had ever made in my life.

By a quarter to one the meal was ready and the table was set. I spruced myself up, changed my clothes and settled myself decoratively on the sofa. Alas, very tired from all the cooking, I inadvertently dozed off. When I woke up, my sitting room was full of people! Apparently I had been sleeping so soundly that I didn't hear Arnold banging on the door and he and the janitor had had to break it down. The noise had attracted everyone who lived in the building and the janitor, standing with his tools in the hallway, had told the circle of bystanders, "Poor young woman, she must have poisoned herself with gas…."

Needless to say, the lunch was not a flaming success. The chicken turned out to be a touch too crisp. The visiting gentleman remarked that even though he was thirty-five and not married yet, after this experience, maybe he would wait a little longer.

After this fiasco, I wasn't allowed to do anything in the house – not even wash dishes. Instead, until my mother-in-law found us a maid, I had to go to the office with Arnold so that he could keep an eye on me. Fortunately, it didn't take long to find someone – my mother-in-law had a wonderful girl named Mary working for her and her sister, Andulka, was able to come right away.

We settled into a regular routine. Every Friday evening we would go to my in-laws house for dinner. By then, all their children were married. Arnold's oldest brother, Egon, was married to a woman named Inka and they had a three-year-old son, Tomy. His brother, Franta, who was the second-eldest, had married Vlasta in February 1933, the same year that Arnold and I were married, and they didn't have children. Arnold's only sister, Greta, the next oldest, was married to a dentist, Dr. Armin Knopfelmacher, who was like a brother to us. We all had a wonderful time together at those Friday-night suppers. On Saturday night, all ten of us would go to a movie. My mother-in-law would get the tickets in advance, usually by Tuesday, and after the movie we often went to the fashionable Café Boulevard on the main square, Václavské náměstí (Wenceslas Square).

In the early summer I found out that I was pregnant. I remember the first time I felt my son moving around inside me – it was on October 23, 1933. He was a big baby. I was huge and during the last month of my pregnancy, I had to buy men's sandals because my feet were so swollen. Arnold and I were both thrilled when Milan was born on March 23, 1934, weighing 4.5 kilograms. His cousin, Harry Knopfelmacher, Greta and Armin's son, had come into the world earlier that same night. Harry was born at 2:30 in the morning and Milan was born six hours later, at 8:30. It was a very busy night – the Voticky grandparents got two grandsons on the same day! Almost three years later, on January 19, 1937, our daughter, Vera, was born.

In the summer the whole family would go to the spa town of Marienbad about 150 kilometres west of Prague – the women and children stayed all summer and the men came to join us on the weekends. In the winter we would go skiing in Spindelmühle in the Giant Mountains on the border with Poland. We were happy with our life and we thought this happiness would last forever. I wasn't the slightest bit aware of the clouds gathering over the horizon.

The Gathering Storm

When Hitler became chancellor of Germany in 1933, we were pre-occupied with all our family weddings. The situation for Jews in Germany steadily deteriorated throughout 1934 with demonstrations, increasing legal and professional restrictions and, finally, the anti-Jewish Nuremberg Laws passed in 1935, but I was a happy and pampered young wife and mother.[1] People talked about it but, to me, the events abroad were just a whisper in the wind. Who had time for politics?

In July 1934, the Austrian chancellor Engelbert Dollfuss was shot during an unsuccessful Nazi takeover. I didn't think about where these events would lead, but I couldn't help being appalled by the thought that the rebels could watch Dollfuss bleed to death, not adhering to his plea for a doctor to be called. The assassination was shocking and quite incomprehensible. Kurt von Schuschnigg succeeded Dollfuss after his death.[2]

---

1 The Nuremberg Laws, announced in September 1935 at the Nazi party rally in that city, legalized discrimination against Jews. For more information, see the glossary.
2 Austrian chancellor Engelbert Dollfuss had established a fascist regime, banned the Austrian Nazi Party and formed an alliance with Italian fascist dictator Benito Mussolini in an attempt to block Hitler's planned takeover of Austria. On July 25, 1934, a group of Austrian Nazis seized the chancellery in an effort to form their own

My husband followed the events on the radio every day. We also befriended the Diamond family from Germany, who brought us even closer to the events unfolding in their country. They came to Czechoslovakia for holidays in the mid-1930s and we spent part of every summer together. They had two beautiful daughters and hoped that my brother Erna would marry one of them. The Diamonds liked Czechoslovakia and as conditions in Germany worsened for Jews, they were looking for a safe haven. Even at this early stage, however, Arnold believed that they would have to cross the ocean to be truly safe. The last we heard of the family was that they had left Germany for Holland, which was still at that time – prior to the Nazi invasion of 1940 – a place of decency and democracy.

In 1935, events began to accelerate. That year, the Nazi minister of propaganda and close associate of Hitler, Joseph Goebbels, called a press conference to announce that Germany was building an army and air force in contradiction to the Versailles treaty.[3] Winston Churchill – who was then a British Conservative member of parliament – seemed to be the only voice of reason, warning the world about the danger of a rearmed Germany. Over the course of the next few years, however, people in Czechoslovakia were listening. I remember that we bought gas masks but we couldn't get ones for the children and I insisted that I wouldn't use one until I could find a child-sized one for Milan. We did manage to get him one but, later, when we needed another for Vera, there weren't any small enough for babies. Again, I insisted that the safety of the children came first. Someone invented

---

government, which resulted in Dollfuss's assassination. His successor, Kurt von Schuschnigg, held power until the German invasion and annexation of Austria on March 12, 1938.

3   The Treaty of Versailles that ended World War I forbade Germany to rearm. The Nazis' 1935 announcement was met with protests from Italy, Britain and France but nothing was done to curtail the German rearmament program. For more information on German rearmament and the Treaty of Versailles, see the glossary.

gas "bags" for babies – when sealed almost entirely into the mask and straps, the infant was very protected. So many people wanted them that they were very hard to come by.

Hitler advanced his agenda in increments. In 1936, the newly established German army marched into the Rhineland, a special demilitarized zone since the end of World War I, and thereby created a situation in which the German soldiers guarded the north shore of the river while the French army guarded the south shore. The world expected France to object, but Hitler gained all this territory without firing a single shot. The French parliament met and there were speeches, but nothing happened.[4] People were shocked at the news. The newspapers in 1936 also ran stories about the Italians using poison gas against the Ethiopians and about the civil war in Spain.[5] The Olympic Games took place in Germany in 1936 – for the duration of the games, all the anti-Jewish signs suddenly disappeared and Germany seemed to be a friendly and hospitable place. In my world, though, nothing much had changed. I was expecting my second child and was happy when my baby girl was born.

Suddenly, events came even closer to home. In the fall of 1937, German Jews who had been released from the Dachau concentration camp started arriving in Prague; they had been able to leave Germany with the help of American Jews.[6] My brother-in-law Armin

---

4 For more information on the Rhineland Crisis of 1936, see the glossary.

5 For more information on the Italo-Abyssinian War and the Spanish Civil War, see their glossary entries.

6 Dachau, just outside Munich in southern Germany, was the first Nazi concentration camp. Initially constructed in March 1933 to house political opponents of the Nazi regime, the camp inmates also included Jews who were arrested for being communists, socialists, trade union organizers or, after 1935, for contravening the Nazi racial laws known as the Nuremberg Laws. After their release had been negotiated by the American charitable organization known as the Jewish Joint Distribution Committee (JDC), the Jews and their families were forced to leave Europe as soon as possible and many passed through Czechoslovakia. For more information on Dachau, the Nuremberg Laws and the American Jewish Joint Distribution Committee, see the glossary.

Knopfelmacher was a dentist and repaired some of the inmates' teeth that had been broken in the beatings they had received in the camp. He didn't charge them for the work, feeling that they had already suffered enough. Each one of those refugees had a story to tell. Listening to their stories, as early as 1937, Armin applied for permission to immigrate to the United States.

On September 14, 1937, President Tomáš G. Masaryk died.[7] It was a sad, gray day. Arnold decided to rent an apartment with a window overlooking the Old Town Square just so that we could watch the long funeral procession. Our whole family joined us for the somber occasion.

Then came the fateful year of 1938. By now, everyone was anxiously watching international events unfold. First came the *Anschluss* or annexation of Austria. Germany had been pressuring Austria to agree to become annexed to Germany since 1934, but Austria's leaders had resisted. In February 1938, Hitler invited Austrian Chancellor Schuschnigg and Austrian President Miklas to his mountain retreat at Berchtesgaden and dictated conditions to them, threatening that if they weren't met, his Wehrmacht (German armed forces) would march into Austria. After two days of hard negotiations, the two Austrian leaders accepted Hitler's terms. But Schuschnigg angered the dictator when, on his return, he called a plebiscite on the annexation question. Without consideration of what had previously been agreed to, the German army marched into Austria. At one o'clock in the afternoon on March 12, 1938, Austria was renamed Õstmark and became a part of Germany. Hitler then held his own plebiscite – it's no wonder that under his watchful eye over 90 per cent of Austrians voted *ja* (yes).[8]

---

7 Tomáš Garrigue Masaryk (1850–1937) was the founder and first president of Czechoslovakia. He was known for his strong public opposition to antisemitism.

8 For more on the *Anschluss*, see the glossary.

After the *Anschluss*, another wave of Jewish refugees arrived in Czechoslovakia and told us what was happening in Vienna. Then, the Sudeten crisis, which had been looming over us for years, became acute.[9] By now Milan was four years old and Vera was one and a half. I had to listen to the terrible stories and read about the endless proposals and counterproposals and constant rehashing of what British liberal politician Walter Runciman had reported, what British prime minister Neville Chamberlain and French president Édouard Daladier had said, and what Hitler had done. I couldn't be indifferent to politics anymore. Nevertheless, the things that were being reported from Germany and Austria still seemed incredible to many of us. Arnold was following the events anxiously and we worried about what would happen to Czechoslovakia. The international alliances in place at the time made Czechoslovakia a question of security for all of Western Europe.[10] In those days, people believed in diplomacy; still, as the great powers negotiated for peace in Europe, Czechoslovakia prepared to defend itself. In May 1938, Czechoslovak president Edvard Beneš ordered a partial mobilization.

In September of that year, Hitler held a rally in Nuremberg and incited by his fiery speech, the Sudeten Germans marched through the streets of Sudetenland's main cities, expecting Hitler's army to come in and take over. There were skirmishes and Konrad Henlein,

---

9 The Sudeten area in northwestern Czechoslovakia was home to a large ethnic German population and the Nazis had long-standing intentions to incorporate the area into a Greater Germany. The crisis erupted in April 1938 when Hitler began to advocate on behalf of Sudeten Germans and local ethnic German residents demanded greater autonomy. Months of international negotiations ensued, culminating in the Munich Conference of September 1938 when the Sudeten region was ceded to Germany. For more information, see the glossary.

10 Czechoslovakia was party to several military alliances signed in the 1920s and 1930s – most notably with France (1924) and with the Soviet Union (1935) – that called for mutual assistance in the event of an attack.

the leader of Sudeten Germans, issued a six-hour ultimatum. The Czech government rejected it and the uprising in Sudeten was soon put down by the Czech police and army. Henlein escaped to Nazi Germany.

That evening, to everyone's amazement, the newspaper vendors in Prague were calling, "Extra, extra, read all about it! Prime minister of the powerful British Empire on his way to plead with Hitler!!!" British prime minister Neville Chamberlain began his negotiations with Hitler on September 15 at Berchtesgaden. Hitler insisted that the Sudeten region be given to Germany. After two days, Chamberlain began putting pressure on Czech President Beneš. When the other great powers joined in, the Czechoslovak government yielded. The Czechoslovak people, however, did not – they demonstrated in large numbers and in the wake of these demonstrations, the government fell.

On September 22, another discussion opened in Bad Godesberg, a municipal district of Bonn in west-central Germany. This time, Hitler upped the ante by also presenting demands for territory from Poland and Hungary. Chamberlain wanted an international commission to oversee the withdrawal of the Czechoslovak army, but Hitler would have none of that. The British prime minister also asked for an international guarantee for the remaining part of Czechoslovakia. Hitler acceded to this demand, but secret plans that later came to light revealed that he had never intended to keep those promises.

The Czechoslovak government rejected the Godesberg agreement between Hitler and Chamberlain, and President Beneš ordered a full mobilization. On September 29, 1938, four European powers – Germany, Britain, France and Italy – met at a conference in Munich. The four chief negotiators were Chamberlain, Daladier, Mussolini and Hitler. Czechs were not invited but they came anyway. On September 30, half an hour after midnight, the four powers signed an agreement that the Sudeten region would be surrendered to Germany. The same day, an international commission began its work determining the fate of the rest of Czechoslovakia. So Hitler got everything he wanted –

again without a fight. When he returned to Britain, Chamberlain uttered his infamous declaration that he had brokered a deal for "peace for our time."

The women and children in our family and circle of friends spent that summer in a castle in the south, near the disputed Sudeten area, that belonged to one of Arnold's business friends. Egon, Franta and Armin had been called up for military service as a result of the mobilization and Arnold came on weekends. In those days, with the threat of imminent war hanging over us, it seemed prudent to move from the capital to the countryside. I remember how depressed we were after the Munich accord was signed. We could see the stunned soldiers, complete disbelief on their faces, leaving the fortifications that they had been so determined to defend before our country had been forced to surrender the Sudetenland.

We felt that we had to do something, anything, rather than just watch helplessly, so we set to work. We made soup in huge pots that we found in the castle kitchen, put up tables by the side of the road and served the steaming soup to the retreating soldiers. It was little more than a gesture, but sharing in the common misery made us feel a little better. Everyone was reading the daily papers and listening to the news, but although we knew what was happening, a normal mind couldn't imagine the horrors that were ahead of us.

After the occupation of the Sudetenland, Czechoslovakia was even more crowded with refugees. There was a feeling of looming danger, especially among the Jews, and many began desperately looking for a safe haven. Derogatory publications directed against Jews started to appear in Prague. A new sign hanging from the top floor of a tall building dominated the main square with the cryptic message "Svůj k svému." (To each his own.) It was offensive to people who were being threatened with persecution. Such evidence of hatred, ubiquitous in Nazi Germany, would have been unthinkable in the republic of Tomáš Masaryk, and unimaginable before Munich.

Arnold saw the signs. In early 1938, he had applied for papers to go to America. My mother's brother Emil was already living in Chicago. He had issued eighteen affidavits to support his relatives' applications to immigrate to America, but of all of those, only four people made it to Chicago. The lucky ones were the family of my late uncle Zigmund Kohn from Vienna – his wife, Irma, his daughter, Edith and her husband, and his son, Franta. When Franta Kohn left Vienna for the US during the eventful summer of 1938, customs officials kept turning him back at the Czechoslovak border, even though he already had his affidavit to Chicago. Our small republic was already overrun with refugees. Franta tried to cross the border a few more times but always in vain until my brother Erna took the train to Bratislava, settled the matter with the customs agents and brought Franta to Prague. Franta stayed with us for several months as our guest.

Some time before Franta left Prague for Chicago, Arnold had sent seven thick albums of his valuable collection of precious stamps to Holland with professional smugglers. He asked Franta to pick them up in Amsterdam and let him know by telegram when he had them. Arnold wanted him to take them to safety in America. When Franta arrived in Amsterdam, he sent a telegram confirming that he had the seven "shirts." In 1943, after we ourselves had managed to leave Czechoslovakia for safety, Arnold wrote to Franta and asked him to send back the stamps. Franta kept procrastinating and in the end only ever sent us two books – the smallest and least valuable ones. He and his family had simply stolen the rest – they hadn't expected us to survive.

My mother was terribly humiliated by their behaviour. These people were her relatives! She wrote them a strongly worded letter in which she renounced and condemned them for what they had done. We later learned that Irma had travelled back to Europe when the war ended to sell the cinema they owned in the Seventh District of Vienna, the Kino UHU. She returned to the US by boat and died when she arrived in New York. Franta had died during the war of a heart attack. He was only about forty years old.

~

November 9, 1938, was the infamous night now known as Kristall-nacht.[11] This supposedly spontaneous demonstration against Jews in all the Nazi-occupied lands was, in reality, carefully planned. The world was shocked by the vicious display of hatred and violence, and there were protests from the free world. England subsequently offered a haven for Jewish children called the Kindertransport.[12] Our son Milan and his cousin Harry, both only four years old, were registered to go but we changed our minds about letting such small children go and took them off the list.

Many Germans were shocked by the destruction and brutality as well and the Nazis realized that such an event should not be repeated – at least not under public scrutiny. Some people didn't approve when they saw a kindly neighbourhood merchant being beaten up, but there were others who felt that it should be done, but out of the public view. The latter was the official belief that the Nazis held until the end.

Not long after Arnold and I were married, he had opened a jewellery store in partnership with my brother Erna. Before Christmas 1938, my husband decided to close the jewellery business in Prague and sold it for next to nothing to the brother of his friend, Cenek Sykora. The transfer took effect on January 1, 1939. Arnold made this decision on the spur of the moment after an incident with a beggar. Arnold had regularly maintained the practice of distributing alms from the store on Fridays. On this particular occasion, the beggar in-

---

11 Literally the "Night of Broken Glass," Kristallnacht was a series of pogroms that took place in Germany and Austria on November 9–10, 1938. For more information, see the glossary.

12 The Kindertransport (Children's Transport) was a government-sanctioned but privately financed initiative to bring German Jewish children to Britain that rescued nearly 10,000 children under the age of seventeen between December 1938 and September 1939. For more information, see the glossary.

solently demanded more. In response, Arnold calmly and silently slid the money back into the drawer. The beggar went to the store entrance and screamed into the busy street that the Jew was beating him. A big crowd gathered, but fortunately, some police officers who knew my husband picked up the beggar and quickly ended the whole incident. But to Arnold, this was another clear sign that times were changing and that what was left of the republic would not last much longer.

How the police knew my husband is another interesting story. The police in Prague were very good at making sure that stolen jewellery was not sold in stores, and they would keep all the jewellers informed about stolen goods so that they could keep an eye out for them. Arnold had recently purchased some jewellery from a man in accordance with his normal business practice of holding the merchandise for a period of time and paying the seller later. Soon after Arnold had accepted the jewellery, the police came around and told him about a new batch of stolen jewellery taken by a thief whose modus operandi was to romance wealthy American divorcées on vacation in Prague and then steal their jewellery. I walked into Arnold's office in the back of the store while the two detectives were talking to him about it and told them that I remembered seeing the man. When the time came for the thief to collect his money, he sent a taxi driver to pick it up and the police had me go with them to follow the taxi and identify him. We spotted him sitting at a café and the police arrested him. That was another one of my short careers – detective.

At the end of February 1939, Arnold sent my brother Vilda, who was a lawyer and not married, to Switzerland to arrange some money matters for him – Arnold had sent money and jewellery out of the country through people who were paid twenty-five cents for every dollar they smuggled out. Vilda was to wait in Switzerland to receive that money from the couriers and then deposit it in a Swiss bank. When my brother called to say that he was coming home because everything had been accomplished, Arnold told him to stay a few more days. He was lucky – a few days later, on March 15, 1939, the Nazis occupied Czechoslovakia. At least one of us was in the free world.

Searching for Shelter

The day that the last remaining island of democracy in Central Europe disappeared was depressing and unforgettable. It confirmed that my husband had been right in his efforts to leave. "Go anywhere," he would tell people, "go as far as possible."

On that terrible Wednesday, March 15, 1939, Andulka woke me up at six in the morning and told me that Hitler's troops were on their way to Prague. We got up and I asked her to pack a suitcase for my husband and me. The nanny was to pack a suitcase for the children. Without discussion, we decided to go to my parents.

While she was packing, Andulka came to me and asked, "Madam, should I pack the silver too?" I told her not to, but I was to relive this small and seemingly insignificant moment almost sixty years later in Montreal. On January 17, 1994 – I remember the date exactly – there was an exceptionally devastating earthquake in Los Angeles and I was watching the news coverage on television in my apartment. On the screen, a black woman sifted through the remnants of her home, lamenting, "My house, my house…." At that moment, I had a vivid flashback – there, in my sitting room in Montreal, completely lifelike, was Andulka, asking me that question about the silver. She looked just the way I remembered her and spoke so clearly that I thought I was losing my mind. It was so upsetting that I needed professional help to calm me down.

Our nanny, who was an ardent Czech patriot from Sudeten, was so unnerved by the events that while running down the stairs she fell and broke her right arm. "I would be of no use to you now," she said to me before she left to stay with her parents. We arranged for Andulka to come to my parents' house every morning to help with the children.

We had left our home in such a hurry that we hadn't even had a chance to tell my parents that we were coming. It's interesting to see how our family's sense of togetherness immediately came into play. Our car was parked in front of my parents' building and an hour later, my brother arrived with his wife, Hilda, and their baby, Eva. Erna and Hilda had gotten married on October 28, 1937, and their first daughter, Eva, was born a year later on October 29, 1938. We had all instinctively gathered there, without having called each other first. From that day on, we lived in my parents' apartment on 18 Celetná Street, in the centre of Prague – it was upstairs from the jewellery store that Arnold had owned. As soon as we arrived, Arnold left the house to try to get exit visas for all of us. He came back that afternoon, discouraged because he had only managed to secure one exit visa – for himself. He had paid 50,000 Czech korun for it, which wasn't very much – by that time, the exchange rate had dropped from around thirty korun to the US dollar to 600 korun to the dollar – so it was only about $83 US. The exit visa was valid for ten days, but in the end he had to let it expire because he wouldn't leave without the rest of the family.

Three families were now living in that one apartment. We were so crowded that we even had to use the bathroom for other purposes. When we needed an extra bed, we put a sheet of plywood over the bathtub to create a platform for it and on other occasions, a smaller sheet of plywood turned the bathtub into a card table so that Arnold, Erna, Liza and her friend Helena Ganzova could play cards far into the night without disturbing anyone. At least it took their minds off our unhappy situation.

Helena was a schoolmate of Liza's and a frequent visitor to our home. She was the daughter of a prominent family from Hradec Králové, about 115 kilometres away in Bohemia. She was in Prague studying social work, and she and Liza had quickly become friends. In better times, the two girls had attended a boarding school in Praha-Vršovice, a district of Prague that is about one and a half kilometres south of the city centre. Her father, a fine and dignified doctor, visited his daughter every time he was in Prague and on such occasions would take her and some of her friends out for a nice lunch. He must have worried about his daughter, alone in a big city, and about whether these young ladies were kind to her. So one day, while he was at lunch with a few of his daughter's schoolmates, he decided to make sure and asked them directly, "Ladies," he asked, "are you kind to my Helenka?" I was so touched when Liza told me this story. "Helenka" had a pampered childhood but she didn't have much happiness in her later life.

~

Our homeland was now called the "Reichsprotektorat Böhmen und Mähren" (Protectorate of Bohemia and Moravia) and we were all subject to the mad and ever-changing rules and regulations of Hitler's Germany.[1] We were now desperate to find a safe haven. We started going from one consulate in Prague to another and Vilda did the same in Zurich. We already had passports for travelling abroad and both Milan and Vera were included on mine, but we also needed exit visas and visas from the receiving country. As soon as the consular officials found out that we were Jewish, they refused to give us visas. But we kept trying.

1   On March 15, 1939, following the invasion of Czechoslovakia, Nazi Germany established the Protectorate of Bohemia and Moravia and Czech Silesia (what is now the Czech Republic) and granted limited independence to a new Slovak Republic.

In early April 1939, we tried in vain to get to Yugoslavia when we received a letter from an aristocratic lawyer, Mr. Vujic, inviting the whole family – eleven people – to his home in Zagreb.

Our acquaintance with Mr. Vujic dated back to the summer of 1938, when we were in Yugoslavia with my sister for the holidays. We met this gentleman on the beach, and he ended up proposing to Liza. She made no promises, but that October he came to Prague to formally ask my parents for her hand. Liza was still in school then and told her ardent suitor that she would make her decision after graduation. When he wrote that letter in 1939, he was still waiting for her answer. His offer to bring the whole family to Zagreb was very generous indeed. Arnold and my brother Erna had gone to the Yugoslav consulate to get visas, but were told that they could only get them if they had birth certificates proving that they weren't Jewish.

They went to the Protestant church on Staroměstské náměstí (Old Town Square) called the Czechoslovakian Church, where the followers of Jan Hus worshipped.[2] They talked to one of the clerics there who agreed to issue the required certificates for 1,000 korun each. They took the papers back to the consulate, but this time the official told them that they weren't acceptable, that they would only be valid if they were dated at the time of birth. Back to the church they went, but the minister told them that there was nothing he could do. Arnold and Erna had lost more than the money – they both deeply regretted that before they could get the documents from the church, they had had to get certificates from the rabbi in Prague stating that they had relinquished Judaism. They had had no choice. In the greater scheme of things, this had seemed to be a small sacrifice.

After this attempt, I decided to go to the Gestapo to apply for an exit visa for a trip to Italy, giving the excuse that Milan had had

---

2 Jan Hus (1370–1415) was an important fifteenth-century Czech religious reformer whose teachings anticipated the later Lutheran Reformation. He was convicted of heresy and burned at the stake.

his tonsils removed in the winter and the doctor had recommended ocean air for his recuperation.[3] One did not need a visa to enter Italy at this time; I just had to get out. The man at the Gestapo office looked at my passport and then at me and barked, "Arisch?" (Aryan?) I barked back, "Jawohl!" (Yes!) He gave me a pink slip to put in my passport – that was the exit visa that covered both me and the children. When I came home, my husband said that the visa was priceless. "One of us has to start," he said, "I will find a way to get out later – somehow."

On April 29, 1939, the whole family came to see me and the children off at the railway station. It was the first time in my life that I would have to take care of five-year-old Milan and two-year-old Vera all by myself. Everybody was crying and my mother-in-law kept repeating, "You will come back, you will come back...."

The train pulled out of the main railway station in Prague, Wilson Station, at two o'clock in the afternoon and at midnight we had to change trains in Munich. That was difficult because the children were half-asleep and could only stumble along. The second train then continued on to San Remo on the Italian Riviera, where we arrived in the late afternoon and took a taxi to our hotel. We had supper in our room and then I gave the children a bath and put them to bed. I was tired too, but so lonely and desperate that I spent the whole night writing letters and crying.

I thought that I knew Italy – I had been there a few times as a tourist – but this was different. This time I was a refugee. When I took the children to the beach, I found that it was full of people trying to

---

3   Within months of seizing control of Czechoslovakia, Adolf Eichmann, known as the "architect of the Holocaust," opened a Gestapo (Nazi security police) office in Prague and began implementing anti-Jewish measures similar to those contained in the 1935 Nuremberg Laws – Jews were forced to register for emigration and turn over most of their property in the guise of a compulsory "Jewish emigration tax"; Jewish books and newspapers were banned, and Jews were excluded from economic, cultural and political life. For more information on the Gestapo and the Nuremberg Laws, see the glossary.

get permission to settle somewhere, anywhere – South America, the United States, Canada – anywhere. Since misery loves company, we all got acquainted. Many of my new friends spoke German, which was good because my Italian was poor.

Back in Prague, my husband worried about us. He couldn't find a way to leave Czechoslovakia – Jewish men age eighteen to forty could not get exit visas. So he asked my brother, who was still in Zurich, to come and stay with us so that I wouldn't be alone with the children. I had a hotel suite that was large enough for all of us. Vilda came but he couldn't stay long.

Every day at lunchtime I would leave the children at the table – they were very well-behaved and ate with a knife and fork like grown ups – while I went to the telephone in the hall to call Arnold. When I came back to the table, my new friends could tell that I'd been crying, so they would laugh and make jokes to cheer me up. My Italian friends were very kind. I especially remember a doctor who was there with a small boy the same age as my daughter. The father couldn't understand how it was that my daughter could eat by herself, while his son had to be fed sitting on the nanny's lap.

Time continued to pass and Arnold still couldn't find a way to get out of the "protectorate." I was getting progressively more desperate and would pace on the beach like a mad person.

While I was in Italy, my sister, Liza, was in the last year of her studies in social work at the faculty of social studies in Prague founded by Charlotte Garrigue Masaryk, the Boston-born wife of the republic's first president. By then, alas, the government had already started implementing the order to ban Jewish students from schools and to get around it, the administration of Liza's school allowed the Jewish students to covertly continue their studies outside of the regular classes. In this way, the Jewish students in the graduating class – including Liza and her best friend, Helena Ganzova – were able to mark their proud moment secretly, without any ceremony.

By the middle of July 1939, I decided that I would take my chances and return to Prague. What a crazy idea! It was only after the war that I fully realized how terrible that decision was. At the time, however, I didn't know that unless I got out again – which by then was next to impossible – the children and I would face certain death.

On our way back to Prague, we shared our compartment with an Italian man. He was fluent in German and tried to convince me to leave the train with him in Milan – with the children – and spend some time with him there. In response to this preposterous suggestion, I asked him what he thought I should do with the children. Even for that he had a ready answer. He would hire a nurse, he said. So I asked, "What about my husband waiting at the railway station in Prague?" "Oh, not to worry," said the enterprising fellow, "you can telephone him and tell him that you've been delayed for a few days…." Needless to say, when the train reached Milan, he disembarked by himself.

Two other people boarded in Milan and took his place in our compartment. We got acquainted as soon as they settled in and I learned that they were from Romania. The man was a doctor and he and his wife were returning from Paris. They wanted to find out what I knew about immigrating to France. He spoke to me about politics, but I was careful and kept the real reason why we were in Italy to myself. I just told him that my son had had a tonsil operation and I had taken him to San Remo to recuperate.

At one point I had to leave the compartment to take the children to the bathroom and when I returned the man said to me, "Tell me, are you Jewish?" That surprised me because, with my blond hair and blue eyes, people usually didn't guess. Faced with this direct question, however, I said yes and asked him why he wanted to know. "I knew that you were Jewish," he replied, "because you were taking such good care of your children." I told him then that I was going back to meet my husband so that we could all leave again, that I couldn't bear being in Italy without him. I also advised him and his wife to get out of Romania while there was still time, even if immigrating to France was not ideal. I hope that they listened.

When we arrived home, I found Prague to be a very sad place, much worse than it had been when we left. Still, we were glad to be together. During my absence, the family had dispatched a large wooden container to Chicago, still thinking that we would be able to immigrate there. The "lift" (shipping container) was as large as the size of a room – inside it were three double couches, linens, kitchen utensils and all kinds of other household items.

Liza and I decided that in these uncertain times we needed to learn a trade. Many people tried to learn something that they could do in a foreign land and we found a woman who was an expert knitter to teach us her craft. Her family was from Vienna and had run away to seek safety in Prague after the *Anschluss*. They had a fourth floor apartment on Maiselova Street, near the river Vltava. She taught us diligently all morning, but she was a devoted wife and mother, so at noon, when her husband and son were due home for lunch, we had to be out of there.

Not long after my return to Prague in the summer of 1939, we also began preparing documents to leave, now not for Chicago, where we had been refused, but for England. We secured all the necessary documents from the police and the various ministries and had our medical examinations at the British consulate. Our departure was set for the first week in September and since it was now late August and there was nothing more for us to do, we decided to take a final little holiday.

We stayed in a hotel owned by some people named Zahradnicek in the village of Babice, about thirty kilometres southeast of Prague. Mr. Zahradnicek was the chief of police in Prague and his whole family was very nice to us. They frequently invited us to their home even though they knew that we were Jewish – as I've said, by the summer of 1939 some anti-Jewish measures were already in place. There were some refugees from Austria staying in the same hotel and on one occasion, when I was reprimanding Milan for some transgression, a woman from Vienna said to me, "Let him do what he wants – the child is facing hard times...."

Alas, our carefully made plans came to naught – September 1 came and Germany attacked Poland, and Britain and France declared war on Germany. England was now closed to us. We had to start all over again. Vilda, who was still in Switzerland, kept trying to get us visas to any country, anywhere, but by this time, we were required to have our passports stamped with a J – for "Jew." As soon as any of the consulates saw the J, they would turn us down.[4] And, as before, even though it was possible to get an exit visa from the protectorate authorities, they still refused to give them to Jewish men age eighteen to forty, so Arnold couldn't leave. We kept trying anyway.

One day in October I went shopping for food early in the morning. When I got back, our maid, Mana, met me at the door and whispered, "The Gestapo are here!" I hurried first to the sitting room, where my husband kept his remaining collection of stamps – they were less valuable than the books he had sent to Holland, but they still had some worth. I asked the maid to take them downstairs to the store – which, of course, didn't belong to us anymore.

After Mana took the stamps out of the apartment I went into my father's den, where I found five Gestapo men. Everything was in disarray – desk drawers had been pulled out and the contents scattered; papers and books were on the floor. In my perfect German I asked, "What are the gentlemen looking for?" They didn't answer.

I realized that my husband wasn't there and that he was probably still in bed in his pyjamas – after all, it was eight o'clock in the morning. I quickly went to our room and got him a coat, a pair of pants and some shoes. "When I cough," I told him, "you run!" I stood between the entrance to the den and the sitting room and when I saw that he was dressed and that nobody was watching, I started to

---

4 At Switzerland's request – in order to limit Jewish immigration – Germany began stamping German Jewish passports with a red J in October 1938. When Anka took her children to Italy in April 1939, the law requiring that Czech Jews have their passports stamped with a J had not yet come into effect.

cough. Arnold ran out of the apartment and down the stairs to the store that now belonged to Mr. Sykora. He got out in the nick of time – the Gestapo continued to search the whole apartment. When they entered the sitting room, they went directly to the place the stamp collection had been kept. They must have been able to see that something had been taken out of there.

The Gestapo officers decided to take my father with them and I began behaving like a crazy person. I ran around screaming, then grabbed a chair and threw it at the whole group of men standing together in one corner. There is no doubt in my mind that if the same event had happened six months later, I would have been shot for my actions. Instead, astounded, they turned to my father and asked, "Can't you calm her down?" "Well, no," he said politely, "you can see that she's upset."

During my fit I managed to convey to the intruders that my husband and my brother had left the country and that, as they could see, there were three small children in the apartment. My father was the only one who could support us. However, the Gestapo weren't concerned about the well-being of our children. They couldn't have cared less.

The children were still in their pyjamas. My mother stood there in shock, unable to move, and as the Gestapo led my father away, I called out defiantly, "Long live President Beneš!" One of the officers put his hand over my mouth and whispered in Czech that I had better be quiet or else they would have to take me too. As soon as they closed the door behind them, I took a pair of long underwear from a drawer, opened the window and called out as they were leaving the building, "Wait, wait," and threw the underwear down. It was a cold day in October and I thought that my father might need them. One of the officers looked up and said that he wouldn't need it because he would be back the same evening. Taking a look around our apartment, I found it difficult to believe that.

By six o'clock, though, my father really had come home. He told us that he had been terrified, but when he was taken to the Gestapo office and one of the officers told him, "Sit down Mr. Kanturek," he began to relax a little. He learned that the reason for his arrest was that he had been writing letters to my brother in Zurich every day. The Gestapo didn't know how much of a family man my father was – he lived only for his family and at the end of each day needed all of us gathered around him at the table. The Gestapo, however, viewed these daily letters with suspicion and thought that my father was a spy. But after they interrogated him, they decided to let him go.

~

Since our plans to immigrate to England had been scuttled, we started looking for another possibility. We knew that our cousins Karel and Franta Gross were organizing an illegal transport to Palestine, so the next morning, Arnold and I went to their office.[5] Slavek Polak, another cousin, was also there, along with a man from Vienna named Mandel who was a brother-in-law of my late uncle Zigmund, my mother's brother. The four of them were trying to get people out of the country and we decided to go too. They took our names and in preparation for life in Palestine I went shopping for children's clothes in large sizes that Milan and Vera could grow into. Unfortunately, we soon found out that this new plan had fallen through too.

On New Year's Day 1940, we were still living together in my parents' home. Life was more difficult from day to day because of the anti-Jewish restrictions and there didn't seem to be any hope of getting out. Then, in February, just when we were beginning to feel really hopeless, my brother phoned from Zurich to tell us that he could get us to China. My first reaction was to tell Arnold, "For heaven's sake,

---

5 The authorities in British Mandate Palestine severely limited the number of Jewish immigrants allowed to enter the territory before, during and after World War II. Jewish organizations established a clandestine movement known as Aliyah Bet to bring Jewish immigrants without permits to Palestine.

if we're going to die, let us die here...." I didn't know anything about China. Obviously, I wasn't being very smart, but I had no way of seeing what our future would have been had we stayed in Czechoslovakia.

We received Vilda's phone call on a Monday and on Thursday morning there was a radio announcement that Jewish men age eighteen to forty would now be allowed to leave the protectorate. I realized that we would have to seize the opportunity and said to my husband, "Arnousku, there seems to be no other way – we have to go to China...." Arnold called Vilda and asked him to do everything possible to make the arrangements, the sooner the better.

I started immediately making the rounds of the necessary Nazi government ministries all over again to get exit visas. The official red tape had always been irritating, but what we had to do now was enough to drive a person crazy. One day I came home with an armful of forms that had to be filled out and signed – I sat at the table and signed forty times for myself, then forty times for Milan (Milan Josef Israel Voticky) and forty times for Vera (Vera Sarah Voticky); because the children were both minors I also had to sign each of their forms (Annamarie Sarah Voticky as mother). We had to add the name of Israel to each Jewish male's name and the name Sarah to each Jewish female's name so that we could be more easily identified as Jews. I signed the forms 120 times, endlessly signing, until I started banging my head on the table. Everyone gathered around me, trying to calm me down. My parents kept saying, "It's nothing, it's all right, it's ridiculous, but look at the bright side, you are getting out of here...."

In late March 1940, when the time came for us to get our exit visas, my husband came with me to the police headquarters. When we got inside, however, I asked him to stay in the corridor and let me go in by myself. At that point I thought that Arnold, as a Jewish man, was more at risk of being detained than I was – I couldn't even imagine that Jewish women and children were just as vulnerable. Arnold agreed and waited in the hallway, pale with fear for me. I took out a 1,000 korun banknote and placed it inside my passport, then marched into the office and put the passport on the desk. The official at the counter slid the money deftly into the desk drawer and stamped the document – much relieved, with the stamped trophy in my hand, I turned and left the room.

But the hardest part was still to come – we now had to go to the Gestapo office in the affluent Dejvice district in downtown Prague. It was located in a villa that had been confiscated from the Weinmann family, wealthy Jewish financiers and coal mine owners. There was another Gestapo office on Panská Street in the centre of Prague, in a building that had been confiscated from a family of wealthy bankers, the Petscheks. Taken over by the Gestapo, it was transformed into the sinister building known as "Pečkárna" – a place where people were killed. Just being in the vicinity of Gestapo offices was dangerous for us. Jewish men had to take off their hats from at least a block away – if they were seen with their heads covered, the Nazi thugs would beat them up. Foolishly we thought that if we came there with two small children, they would be softer on us.

When our turn came and we stood in front of the desk, the Gestapo man closely examined my passport. In the document, where the children were described as having blond hair and blue eyes, he crossed the words out and said, "Jewish children are not blond!" I kept quiet and just told myself, "Never mind him…. Who cares? … Just give me the stamp." He finally did and Arnold and I walked happily all the way home from Dejvice. It was a miracle to have the exit papers for me and the children. We could really appreciate the significance of it because of all of our experiences with how hard it was to secure them.

All that was now behind us – we had the precious exit visas. We could go to China! About a week later, on Saturday, April 6, 1940, at eleven o'clock in the evening, we left Prague. There were ten of us – me, Arnold, Milan and Vera; my brother Erna, his wife, Hilda, and their daughter, Eva; and my girlfriend Lidka Winter, her husband, Rudla, and their daughter, Eva. My parents and Liza had decided not to come with us – we all believed that elderly people would be safe from the Nazis, as would Liza as a professional social worker. Hermina Müller, my sister-in-law's mother, came with us part of the way and my sister, Liza, and Aunt Heda, my father's sister, accompanied us as far as Brno. My aunt Heda – whom I looked very much like – was an exceptional cook and made the most wonderful pastries. On the train, as a parting present, she gave me some of her recipes. I still use them even now, and every time I do I think of my dear aunt and of that very last time I saw her.

I have an indelible memory of this fateful journey. Hilda's mother, Mrs. Müller, left the train when we stopped in Pardubice and we watched her standing alone on the dark, deserted station platform howling in agony. The sound of her crying haunts me to this day. By the time we got to Brno, where Liza and Heda left us, we were all crying bitterly.

Early the next morning we arrived at the train station in Vienna, so familiar to us in the past. Then the train took us through the Austrian countryside, past picturesque villages, so similar to the ones we knew at home. When we reached the Italian border and the SS men guarding the train got off, everybody else was cheering and jumping up and down, but we were too exhausted and emotionally drained to feel anything at all.[6] By midnight, our train full of refugees had reached Trieste, Italy. There was an active Jewish community there and some of the local people as well as representatives of international Jewish organizations were waiting for us, offering sleeping accommodations. Arnold declined with thanks, saying that there were people who needed help more than we did. The ten of us went to a hotel.

In the morning, my husband and I went to the Swiss consulate,

---

6 SS is the abbreviation for Schutzstaffel (Defence Corps), the brutal and black-uniformed elite force that wielded enormous police and military power throughout the Third Reich and Nazi-occupied territories. For more information, see the glossary.

where Arnold presented our papers, showing that we had the proper documentation to board the ship the SS *Conte Rosso* on Wednesday, April 10, at five o'clock in the afternoon. We already had our tickets. Without any difficulty, the Swiss consul gave him a transit visa to travel from Italy into Switzerland – he was going to Zurich to meet my brother Vilda and get access to our funds in the bank there. But as soon as Arnold arrived in Zurich, he called to tell me that he was having trouble with the Italian authorities – they didn't want to let him cross the border back to Italy. "The war in Western Europe is imminent," explained the Italian consul.

In desperation, Arnold went back to the Swiss authorities, showed the official in charge the ticket and told him, "I have no choice – if I'm not back, my family will have to go to China without me. I'm staying right here, unless you call the Italians and persuade them to let me in, because I have to be aboard the ship by Wednesday." He finally got permission to leave, but at two o'clock in the afternoon on Wednesday we were all waiting anxiously at the station in Trieste, not knowing whether he would arrive in time. You could have cut the tension with a knife. At last Arnold arrived, having successfully concluded all his business in Zurich. I heaved a sigh of relief and, on schedule at five o'clock in the afternoon on April, 10, 1940, we boarded the *Conte Rosso* and settled into our cabin.

When we went to the dining room for dinner that evening, it was very dark – there weren't any lights because France and England were at war with Germany and ships were in danger from German submarines. I commented to Arnold, "For heaven's sake, there are so many old men aboard – none of them have any hair!" But we didn't talk to any of our fellow passengers that night – we just ate our supper and went to sleep. We saw the same people at breakfast the next morning, however, and discovered that they weren't old – their heads were shaved because they had all been recently released from the Dachau concentration camp. American Jews had paid the Germans three hundred dollars per head for their freedom and the Germans had brought them to the port of Trieste by truck the night before. The Germans released them with only the clothes on their backs – they had no handkerchiefs, no toothbrushes, nothing – and they were obviously starving.

We befriended some of them. When Arnold was leaving Zurich, my brother Vilda had given him a suitcase full of his clothes. These men from Dachau were in such dire need that I distributed the contents of the suitcase among them. One of the men, an architect, had only one leg. I gave him whatever he could use from my brother's suitcase and he told us what had happened to him on Kristallnacht. When the SA came to his apartment he, in accordance with the Geneva Conventions, saluted and gave his rank as an officer in World War I.[7] One of the "brown shirts" hit him so hard that he flew across the room. They beat him up and then took him to Dachau. He was on the ship alone, without his family.

Another man, who was from Holland, heard that my husband was in banking and asked him what he should do with his money when he got to Shanghai. Arnold asked him where the money was and when he heard that it was in Holland, he was astounded. "Why did you leave it there?" he asked, "Why didn't you transfer it to Zurich or some other safe place? Holland is sure to be occupied very soon. Go to the captain right away and tell him that you need to telephone the bank to transfer the money immediately." Alas, the man didn't take the advice and by May 5, 1940, while we were still on board ship, Holland and Belgium were occupied by Nazi Germany. On our first night in Shanghai, this gentleman was found running around the block stark naked and had to be admitted to a mental institution.

These are just two of the many stories we heard on that ship. On

---

7 The SA, or Sturmabteilung, was the paramilitary wing of the Nazi party. The Geneva Conventions are a set of treaties and protocols that set the standards for the humanitarian treatment of victims of war. For more information on the SA and the Geneva Conventions, see the glossary.

our way to Shanghai, we sailed via Venice, the Suez Canal, Aden, Singapore, Manila and Hong Kong. We weren't allowed to leave the ship until we reached Manila – a beautiful city, but very hot. We weren't allowed to set foot on the ground in any of the other ports because as Jews from Nazi-occupied Czechoslovakia, we were now considered to be stateless.[8]

---

8   The 1935 Reich Citizenship Law stripped German Jews of their citizenship, effectively making those who did manage to leave the country "stateless" – i.e. they no longer belonged to any nation-state. Unlike many other countries that refused entry to Jewish refugees from all Nazi-occupied territories on the basis that they no longer had a "home country" to return to, the semi-autonomous US-controlled Philippines did allow some of these "stateless" Jews to both land temporarily and even remain in the country as refugees.

Safe Haven in Shanghai

We arrived in Shanghai on Friday, May 10, 1940, at midnight. When we disembarked from the ship, we entered a small building near the dock, where our papers were processed. After spending a whole month at sea, we were finally on solid ground. There were hundreds of people waiting for us as we left the customs building, refugees from Germany, Austria and Czechoslovakia who were waiting to see if somebody from their city was aboard the ship.[1] They were calling out "Vienna" … "Berlin" … but nobody named Prague. When I stepped out on the street carrying Vera on my arm and holding Milan by the hand while Arnold took care of the luggage, I was greeted in German by the words, "Look at the poor young woman with two small children!" I stopped and called out in a strong voice, "PRAHA!" (PRAGUE!) Only one man answered. His name was Kurt Reitler and I knew him – he used to take religious instruction in the same school as I did and came from my district of Prague, from Karlín.

Now there were sixteen of us in our group, including six children under the age of six and two couples from Vienna we had befriended on the ship, each couple with one child. Later they were very grate-

---

1   About 9,000 German Jews, 4,500 Austrian Jews, 1,000 Polish Jews and 250 Czech Jews arrived in Shanghai as refugees between 1938 and 1941.

ful for our help. Kurt took us to a cafeteria and from there started phoning hotels. Unfortunately there were American military ships docked in the harbour and the soldiers had taken all of the hotel rooms. When I saw his frustration, I told Mr. Reitler that we only needed one room, so that the children could sleep in a bed while the rest of us made do somehow, but it was no use. There was nothing available. By two o'clock in the morning Kurt had started phoning the private homes of people in the Czech and Russian communities and managed to distribute us amongst the families. We all took taxis to go to different parts of that strange city. Our family of four went to the home of Mr. and Mrs. Stembera. He was the leader of the Czech Boy Scouts in Shanghai – Milan later joined his group.

I woke up the next morning to strange singing sounds…."Hai how…." When we got dressed and went downstairs, ready to face a new day, I asked Mr. Stembera at the breakfast table about this constant sing-song sound. He explained that somebody was building a house in the neighbourhood and a Chinese "coolie" – the word used for an unskilled male labourer in Asia at the time – had to make this sound while carrying a load so that the supervisor would know where he was so the labourer couldn't steal his load.

I soon learned that the foreigners did not treat the Chinese people very nicely in their own country. The Chinese servant who worked for us would never look at me, even when I spoke to him. At first I thought that it was because he was shy, but I later found out that a Chinese man was not allowed to look a white woman in the eye. There were other restrictions as well – parks were off limits to a Chinese man unless he worked there and a Chinese *amah* – a female domestic – could only enter a park if she had a white child with her. The foreign residents in Shanghai had many ways to show the Chinese who was master. They didn't like the recently arrived refugees from Europe because, as a rule, we treated the Chinese with more respect.

The next day we found a small hotel on Avenue Joffre – one of the main thoroughfares in the French Concession – moved in and started looking for an apartment.[2] That first week in Shanghai I got a good lesson. When the men left in search of an apartment, we "smart" girls forgot to mark down the name of the hotel when we left for a morning walk. The three of us – Hilda, Lidka and I – plus all the children, walked and walked, looking at all the unusual sights, until we got lost. We didn't speak English, we didn't speak Chinese, and we were completely lost. We asked passersby for directions, but nobody could understand us. Since then, whenever I walk out of a hotel in a strange city, the first thing I do is write down the name of the hotel and the address. In the end, exhausted after much blundering, we somehow found our way back.

After spending a week in the hotel, we found a duplex on Destilano Street, also in the French Concession. It was quite primitive, but it had two apartments. Erna and his family lived downstairs and we lived upstairs. To our shock, we soon found out that our neighbours were Nazis, part of the German fifth column, Hitler's supporters who had settled in foreign countries to give the Third Reich a local foothold for its future expansion. We noticed that every evening two cars would stop in front of the house next door and out would come men with an arrogant manner wearing the brown shirts and high boots of the SA. We knew that we couldn't stay long in that neighbourhood.

One day, after driving up and down the lane on his scooter, Milan came home bewildered and bleeding profusely. He told me that the boy next door had cut his arm. I ran out and saw the boy's mother looking out the window of her house. Angrily, I called out to her, "If you don't punish your son for this, I will." The next day I was in the kitchen, which had a very narrow door, and the neighbours' son put his head through the door and called to me in German, "Perish, you Jewish swine!" I wasn't willing to take that kind of abuse – especially

---

2   The French Concession, an area located in the northwestern part of Shanghai, was conceded to France by China in 1849. For more information, see the glossary.

not after I had just crossed oceans to get away from it. I ran after him but he was more nimble than I was. As he was trying to get into his house, my Chinese cook – who used to work for Europeans and spoke fluent German, so he had understood what the boy had said – called out to the neighbours' servant to not let the boy in the house. The servant blocked the door and I caught the rascal. Angry as I was, I gave him a sound thrashing.

A week later, on a Sunday, we were getting ready to go with the children to the race course – a kind of country club that most of the foreign communities in Shanghai had – where we used to go every Sunday. It was a large field where we could play all kinds of sports and games such as tennis, football, soccer and croquet. Around the perimeter of the field were little cabins with terraces in front that were shielded from the sun by an awning, and under the awnings were chairs for the members. The race course was an important part of each community's social life. Inside the cabin was a kitchen where Chinese servants would prepare drinks and snacks for club members, who sat on the chairs on the terrace.

The race course that we went to was a gathering place for the Czech community. There were many Czech expatriates who had been living in Shanghai for a long time. Some of them worked for Škoda, an automobile manufacturer, and some worked for Bata, a shoe manufacturer. There used to be a Czechoslovak consulate in the city but it had closed in March 1939 after the German occupation of Czechoslovakia.

The French Concession had its own police force and on that particular Sunday, some officers from the French police arrived just as we were about to leave for the race course. They managed to communicate to me that I would have to appear in court the next day because our German neighbours, the insolent boy's parents, were suing me for the medical costs they had incurred while their son was in hospital recovering from the beating I gave him. It was obvious that their sympathies were with us – they were loyal to France and France was at war with Germany. The policeman told us with a delighted smile that they had seen him – he really was black and blue. As soon as the police left, another neighbour, a Russian gentleman whom I had never met before, came over and asked if I spoke French. Since I didn't, he offered to go with me to court. Word had obviously gotten around – the whole foreign community was talking about what had happened.

When we went to court, Milan made a good impression on the judge, even though he was only six years old. He was already enrolled in a French school and wore his navy blue uniform and a beret with the school emblem on it. My doctor, Dr. Grossman, who was a Czech originally from Zlín, where Bata had their huge factory, had given me a bill for treating Milan after the boy next door had cut him. I presented the bill to the court as evidence and told the judge what happened. I also showed him what that boy had done to Milan – his arm had been cut from wrist to shoulder, on the diagonal like a loaf of bread, and Milan still has faintly visible scars to this day. The judge dismissed the case – the arrogant Germans were not well liked there.

After this incident we were eager to move out of that neighbour-hood, away from the brown shirts, and Arnold began looking for an-other, larger house, where we all could live. He found a villa on Frelupt Street in the French Concession that was owned by a wealthy Chinese man who agreed to rent it to us. We needed a large house because we were expecting Vilda to arrive from Switzerland in September 1940 and my parents and Liza to arrive not long after from occupied Czechoslovakia. Once we moved, we never heard from the German neighbours again.

I switched Milan from the French school to a private American school because people in the Czech community advised me that he should learn English first. Vera was still small and she attended the Peter Pan preschool. Our landlord was pleased when Arnold told him that Milan would be attending the American school. He told his son that he was lucky to have a boy about his own age who was in the American school living there so that he could learn English from him. About a year later, however, our disappointed landlord complained to Arnold that Milan spoke Chinese like a native while his own son still didn't know a word of English!

In late 1940 my husband and brother opened a small factory to make costume jewellery. We started with twenty-five workers and the business grew slowly at the beginning, but we had to start somewhere. I hired a Jewish woman, a refugee from Germany, to teach the children German because German was the common language of refugees who had come to Shanghai from different parts of Europe. One very hot and sunny day the Fräulein, as we called the German teacher, came home with the children and told me that Milan already spoke German. When they were walking in the park, he had pointed to a shady spot under a tree and said *kalt* (cold) and then he pointed to a sunny path and said *heiss* (hot). He was evidently hot and wanted to walk in the shade.

We were comfortable in the spacious villa with five Chinese servants, although the wealthy Chinese landlord told Arnold – he never spoke to me – that a house that size would normally need at least ten. These servants worked in the house, but they ate separately in a large lean-to attached to the villa. That was the usual practice in such households. We were slowly getting accustomed to living in China and, more slowly, even to the humid climate.

Some days after we moved into the villa, Hilda and I went downtown by streetcar to go shopping for some kitchen utensils because the lift with all our household goods was still in Chicago. There was a very nice department store called Wing on Nanking Road in the International Settlement.[3] The weather was beautiful and the store

---

3   The British, French and American foreign concessions in Shanghai formed a united municipal council in 1854, but in 1862, the French Concession dropped out. In 1863, the British and American concessions united to become the Shanghai International Settlement and were later joined by other foreign nationals. For more information, see the glossary.

was elegant and interesting, so we spent some time inside just looking around. When we finally decided to leave, we took the stairs down from the third floor rather than the elevator and when we reached the ground floor, we saw to our shock and amazement that the ground floor was flooded.

I panicked. We hadn't been in Shanghai for very long and I didn't know that when it rained there, it really poured. Another peculiarity of the climate was that the more it rained, the hotter it got, and May was the rainy season. Alarmed, I ran back upstairs to call the only person I knew who had a telephone, a Czech woman named Mrs. Riga who was married to a German. She and her husband had lived in Shanghai for many years. She calmed me down and advised me to go back down and call a rickshaw. "The man will wade through the filthy water," she explained. "He will carry you to his rickshaw on his back and take you home." Being carried on the back of a strange man wasn't exactly an inviting thought – the rickshaw drivers were all wet and sweating from the rain and the heat – but we didn't really have any choice. It happened exactly as Mrs. Riga said. The rain had stopped by then, but it took some time for the water to subside. It was the first time we used this means of transportation and it was quite a distance from the International Settlement part of Shanghai to the French Concession. Needless to say, it was quite an experience for us! The man took us to dry land from where we could walk the rest of the way home.

~

My brother Vilda arrived from Switzerland aboard the Italian ship SS *Conte Verde* in September and my parents and my sister arrived about four months later on January 30, 1941. As soon as we had arrived in Shanghai, Arnold had gone to the Czechoslovak consul to ask for advice on the best way to get my parents and my sister out of Europe – his own parents didn't want to leave. They managed to acquire visas through the Japanese vice consul in Lithuania, Chiune

Sugihara.[4] At great peril – we later found out that it was with the help of a German woman and her brother – they had travelled by train from Prague via Berlin, Moscow and Vladivostok and then sailed to the port of Kobe in Japan. Arnold went to meet their ship in Kobe and ended up standing on the wharf waiting for them all day until five o'clock in the afternoon. When he got back to Shanghai he told us that he was arrested ten times by the Japanese police while he was waiting. A white man standing at the harbour all day was conspicuous in wartime and the Japanese suspected him of spying. Every time he showed them his papers and explained why he was there, they would let him go – nonetheless it kept happening over and over again in one day.

When my parents and my sister finally arrived he took them to their ship to sail from Kobe to Shanghai. In the morning, while they were aboard ship, my father told Arnold, "You said that you had secured us a first-class cabin, but I passed by another one that was far more opulent." He led Arnold to the cabin to show him. In my father's mind he was still living in his former world – Arnold had to explain to him that the cabin he was talking about was the captain's quarters.

The Czech community welcomed them in Shanghai. Milda Levy, also a refugee from occupied Czechoslovakia, and a group of friends met their ship in a motorboat. We flew a big Czech flag and Milda played the Czech anthem on his harmonica. We were glad to be together again, but, sadly, we learned that my husband's parents hadn't managed to get out of Prague, nor had my brother-in-law, Armin Knopfelmacher. When we had been preparing to leave Prague, we had asked Armin and his family to come with us, but he had de-

---

4   Japanese vice consul Chiune Sugihara, stationed in Kovno, Lithuania, issued more than 6,000 transit visas to Jews – in direct violation of orders from his government – between July and August 1940. After the Lithuanian consulate closed, Sugihara was briefly stationed in Prague in 1941, where he continued to issue visas to Jews. For more information, see the glossary.

clined. When we said goodbye to them, Armin was still optimistic even though the oppression of Jews in the city was already severe. By this time they couldn't even come to the Masaryk Station to see us off because Jews who didn't have travel documents weren't allowed to be on the street after eight o'clock at night. This was the last time we saw him– he had told us that they were staying because somebody would have to be waiting for us at the railway station when we returned. That never came to pass. The last communication from them was a card with the terse message, "Why didn't you insist?" In 1945 we found out that Armin, Greta and Harry, their nine-year-old son, and Arnold's parents, Hugo and Olga Voticky, had all perished in the Holocaust.

My parents told us what it was like in Prague after we left. The oppression intensified – a curfew had already been in place when we were leaving, but it got worse. Jewish children were no longer allowed to go to school. Jews had limited shopping hours, were not allowed to be in any public places – including theatres, cinemas and parks – and after November 1940 they had to wear a yellow Star of David on their outer garments. In spite of all these restrictions, Liza hadn't wanted to leave Prague. Even as she arrived in Shanghai, travelling with us by taxi from the harbour to the French Concession, she asked me briskly how well-established we were there. When I told her that we were manufacturing costume jewellery but the going was slow, she asked resentfully, "So why did you drag us here?" As soon as we arrived at the villa, Liza walked to the record player and put on a record she had brought with her all the way from Prague, an aria from the opera *Rusalka*, by the Czech composer Antonín Dvořák.

My sister was well-educated, witty and very pretty. She had many suitors and was able to pick and choose among them. She later told me about how the restrictions in Prague had affected their lives and what had happened to her and her boyfriend, Karel Matcha. One evening, she ignored the curfew and went out with Karel. They stopped at the fashionable Café Boulevard on Wenceslas Square that we had all frequented in better times, usually after seeing a movie. They took a table in a remote corner, far away from the entrance, by a window overlooking the square.

Suddenly the Gestapo burst in through the door. They went from table to table to check everyone's identification papers. Liza was frightened and Matcha was as pale as the proverbial sheet. For Liza, the place was off limits – she wasn't wearing a yellow star and her papers would clearly show that she was Jewish. Matcha wasn't Jewish but he would have been picked up just for being there with her. By a stroke of luck, the Gestapo patrol was at the table next to them when somebody called from the door summoning them to an emergency. It was a close call for Liza. Yet still she had asked, "So why did you drag us here?" She never mentioned this ever again, though, when she realized what their fate would have been had they remained in Europe. I was angry with her at the time, but I forgave her and never begrudged her for her comment. We were very close.

Liza also recounted how, in this atmosphere, they had prepared for the long and dangerous journey to Shanghai. They had met a remarkable woman named Ilsa Popperova, who was a friend of our cousin, Karel Gross. Ilsa was German and married to a Jew. While it was still possible, her husband had transferred all his possessions into her name. Then she divorced him and helped him immigrate to the United States. When he was safely in the US, she sold his possessions and found a way to send the money to him. All this had happened before Liza met Ilsa and her brother, who was a German soldier. He was quite smitten with Liza and would have wanted to marry her, which was, under the circumstances, quite impossible – at that time, because of the Nuremberg Race Laws, a German would never have gotten permission to marry a Jew. Besides, Liza wasn't at all ready to get married. Still, this decent young German soldier accompanied Liza and our parents to make sure that they reached Berlin safely and got settled on their train going east, a journey full of danger.

~

Life in Shanghai went on and little by little we got accustomed to living in such a foreign culture with all its unusual aspects. I learned to play the popular Chinese game mahjong and there was even a semblance of social life. We made new friends, among them the former Czechoslovak consul, Major Stepan – who had also been a Czech legionnaire in Russia during World War I – and his wife. After the consulate closed, they stayed in Shanghai as refugees and I played mahjong with his wife. Immediately after our arrival he advised Arnold on how to go about bringing my parents and Liza to Shanghai. As far as we know, Major Stepan and his wife continued to live in Shanghai after the war – they had lived there for many years and it had become their home.

We also developed a bond with Vladimir Taussig, the former military attaché at the consulate, and our dear friends, the Gottwalds. Mr. Gottwald was an executive with Bata and when the war ended, they returned to Czechoslovakia and bought a house in Moravia. We met them again in 1948 in London, when we were all refugees again, but after that we regrettably lost contact with them. The last we heard about them was that the Canadian branch of Bata had sent them to manage the company's interests in Africa. They lived in a strange land again and their children had to travel hundreds of kilometres to attend an English school.

Among our interesting friends were Mrs. Kutschback, whose Czech was a unique international tongue since she managed to use several languages in one sentence, and the sociable Pepik Novotny, an outstanding theatrical makeup artist whose wife was Russian. After the war he returned home, as we did, but when we all left again after 1948 he reproached us vehemently, arguing that he and his wife had left Shanghai just to be with us and now we were leaving them. We later heard that he was working for the National Theater in Prague, a prestigious position indeed. Sadly, we never got to see them again.

The Langers were another couple who had been long-time Czech residents in Shanghai. I played mahjong at their house when we lived in the French Concession and they were very hospitable. We would usually visit for a whole day – after a game we would take a break, sometimes even taking showers on the hot days, and then we would talk while the servants served meals. One day, while I was taking a shower, I inadvertently left my diamond engagement ring in the bathroom. The next day I noticed that it was missing and tried to think where I could have left it. Finally, I called the Langers to ask if it was at their house. Mr. Langer was a gentleman of few words. He picked up the telephone and when he recognized my voice, before I even had a chance to explain what I was calling about, he said, "It's in my pocket."

There was also a large Russian colony in Shanghai, people who had been there since 1917 and were refugees from the Russian Revolution.[5] They had had their own difficult experiences, so they sympathized with the newcomers. Complete strangers from the Russian community would offer help whenever they saw that help was needed. Milan went to school with a boy named Mike Fingerut – his mother was Russian and his father was a Russian Jew. We became very good friends and I also used to go to their house to play mahjong.

We had many good friends in Shanghai, interesting people all of them, but with the passage of time, most of their names have evaporated from my memory. We would all meet on Saturdays – the old Czech residents as well as the new Czech refugees – at Czech House, our community's gathering place in the French Concession. Times were not the best they had ever been, but they were far better than they could have been.

---

5   Thousands of Russians, both Jews and non-Jews, fled to Manchuria in northeast Asia after the 1917 October Revolution. When the Japanese occupied Manchuria in 1931-1932, many of them moved south to Shanghai.

The War Reaches Us

On December 7, 1941, Japan attacked Pearl Harbor and everything changed. Relations between the United States and Japan had been deteriorating since the late 1930s and now that the US had entered the war, American and British families were forced into internment camps and their businesses closed.[1] As a result, many of our fellow refugees lost their means of earning a living.

One December evening we heard a knock on the front gate of our villa. When we opened it, we found our friend Vladimir Taussig standing there. He was running from the Japanese, he told us, and asked if we could hide him. He ended up staying with us until he was evacuated to England in January 1942 and after the war he married and settled in the United States.

New Year's Eve 1941 was a sad affair indeed. The old Czech colony members and new refugees all got together at Czech House, but the

---

1 Prior to the attack on Pearl Harbor, the Japanese only occupied the Chinese-administered parts of Shanghai outside the International Settlement and the French Concession. The day after the attack on Pearl Harbor, with the American entry into the war on the side of the Allies, the Japanese occupied the International Settlement and the French Concession. American, British and Dutch residents become enemy nationals overnight, who were registered, identified with red armbands and, beginning in early 1943, sent to a number of internment camps in Shanghai.

gathering was more like a funeral than a party. There was nothing but uncertainty ahead and many of the young men had lost their jobs and were facing a bleak future. The room was full but there was no cheer. I wasn't accustomed to alcohol, but a full decanter of whiskey stood in front of me on the table and I drank it all. I soon began feeling the effects. Our situation suddenly seemed far less dreary and then the room began turning and tilting before my eyes. Arnold got me home somehow and my mother helped him undress me and put me to bed to sleep it off. I was terribly sick the next morning. Taussig heard my moaning and barged into our room with Alka-Seltzer to help cure me. The good fellow had some experience in these matters because in this climate, where tropical infections were rampant, many people drank alcohol thinking that it was a preventive measure.

Overall, compared to their treatment of the American and British residents, the Japanese were fairly decent toward the Jews. It may have been in part because they overestimated the influence that Jews had in Western politics, particularly in the United States. The educated Japanese also still remembered the help that Jewish-American financier Jacob H. Schiff gave Japan when he gave the Japanese government a loan during the 1904 Russo-Japanese war after rejecting a similar request made by Czar Nicholas II.

Nonetheless, we experienced a constant feeling of insecurity after the attack on Pearl Harbor – all kinds of unconfirmed rumours were circulating among the refugees. In 1941, there was new information that the Germans were pressuring their Japanese allies to take drastic measures against the Jews in Shanghai. In January 1942, we heard that SS leader Heinrich Himmler was sending Josef Meisinger, former chief of the Gestapo in Warsaw, to Shanghai.[2]

----

2 Colonel Josef Meisinger, the chief Gestapo representative to Japan, arrived in Shanghai in July 1942, with instructions to carry out the "Final Solution against the Jews" there. It was never implemented because, although the Japanese were allied with Germany, they did not share the Nazis' murderous hatred of Jews.

The Japanese weren't particularly receptive to the German suggestions but in order to appease them, they issued a proclamation on February 18, 1943, that all Jews who had arrived in Shanghai after 1937 would have to move to the district of Hongkew, the poorest and most crowded area in Shanghai. The proclamation creating the ghetto was to take effect three months later, on May 18.

Gestapo emissary Josef Meisinger and his assistants weren't satisfied with this measure alone. They wanted to reach a "final solution" to their perceived problem – the Jews. As the head of the Nazi delegation, Meisinger reportedly suggested that the Jewish population of Shanghai, about 18,000 people, be loaded onto flimsy dinghies without motors or rudders, towed out to sea and left to perish. The Nazis evidently planned to exterminate Jewish people everywhere in the world that they could exert their influence. There were rumours that they had plans to build a death camp with gas chambers on Tsungming Island (Chongming Dao) in the Yangtze delta. In fact, when the first refugees moved into the ghetto, they were told not to unpack because they would be moving on.

The Japanese authorities wouldn't go along with Meisinger's plan for the total annihilation of the Jews, but upheld the order requiring Jews to move to a ghetto. It hit the Jewish community like a thunderbolt – affluent families had been relatively comfortable in Shanghai up to this point. The eleven of us who were living in a large rented villa in the French Concession attended by Chinese servants would now have to move into the newly designated Jewish ghetto in Hongkew. Once an American colony, Hongkew had been a place of great prestige from 1932 to 1937, but had been destroyed during the Japan-China War.[3] When the Chinese troops retreated, the quarter

---

3 The Hongkew (Hongkou) district, situated north and east of the Suzhou Creek, was settled by American colonists in 1848, when it was known as the American Concession. For more information, see the glossary.

was left in ruins, dilapidated and overcrowded. There were clearly not enough homes there for 18,000 Jewish refugees. It was also not clear what would happen to their businesses, jobs, apartments and schools if the Jews were to be truly isolated.

The Japanese let us know that they were willing to trade small rooms in Hongkew for large houses in other parts of the city. "I small, you big," they would say and then touch your nose – that was how the trade was communicated. When the proclamation was first made public I had told Arnold that I wanted to see if I could find a flat in the ghetto. Even without knowing Hongkew I understood that it would be difficult to find a place large enough for all eleven of us. Arnold told me not to go – he said that I would faint if I saw the place. Thousands of poor Chinese lived there in dire, unimaginable poverty. I remember one Chinese family dwelling that had been slapped together from mud in the shape of an igloo. People could only get into it by crawling on all fours through a small opening. I also saw a Chinese dwelling that consisted of one small room divided horizontally – the family lived, cooked and ate in the lower half, while they slept in the upper half.

Chinese families were close, respectful and loving, but the poverty in Hongkew was devastating – an event like a funeral placed an unbearable burden on families. When a person died at home, the family would lay the body outside, in front of their dwelling, until the next morning, when the lifeless bundles were collected in a car. When family members were near death, the families would often take them out to a vacant lot, make them as comfortable as they could and leave them among the flies until they died. Sometimes it took a week, or even longer if the family had miscalculated. After we moved to the ghetto, Milan had to pass by this lot every day on his way to school.

～

Once we knew that we couldn't find a house large enough for all of us in Hongkew we decided that we had no choice but to build one.

Arnold hired a Chinese contractor to construct a house in the row-style of a small motel – a room, a bathroom and another room, then a kitchen, a room, a bathroom and a room – on a lot at 592 Tong Shan Road. As a social worker and nurse, Liza's medical skills were much in demand and she could have been evacuated to England with the British expeditionary forces before the move to the ghetto, but she didn't want to leave without the rest of us.

As the deadline to move to the ghetto approached at the end of May 1943, several young Czech men I used to invite over to have an occasional meal came up with a plan to make their way to Palestine and enlist to fight alongside the British. When they were getting ready for the journey, I bought each of them a pair of thick white socks to wear inside their heavy army boots for good luck and Arnold offered them a piece of good advice: "Fight by all means, but never volunteer for anything!" I don't know how much luck came from my present of white socks and how much from Arnold's advice, but all these fellows managed to reach Palestine, join the army and come through the war alive.

When the time came for us to move to the ghetto, our house in Hongkew wasn't ready – we needed two more months to complete it. In the meantime, we had to have someplace to stay. Fortunately, Arnold's business friends came to our rescue and let us use their house in Hongkew. One of the reasons that our house wasn't ready was that there was trouble on the building site – the work had stopped due to a money dispute between the workers and the contractor. Arnold had duly paid the contractor, but he, in turn, was not paying for the building materials or the workers' wages.

The workers finally rebelled. At least a hundred of them showed up one particular morning with two-wheeled carts, angrily shouting as they proceeded to fill the carts with boards and other building materials. As my luck would have it, I had just arrived to see Arnold at the construction site. I was standing alone in a crowd of Chinese workmen, having no idea what the commotion was about, when a stranger, an expatriate Russian, yelled out to me from the crowd that I should stay absolutely still or the workers would kill me. My husband was also in the middle of it and Milan, the nine-year-old mediator, was translating the workers' demands.

The police came and took away the contractor and the whole crowd followed. Arnold went into the police station and when he came out he was as white as a sheet. He made his way through the melee to me and told me that the police were beating up the contractor and that there was blood everywhere. Eventually, the contractor paid up, the workers returned the building materials, a new contractor was appointed and the work continued. On that day, though, there was no question that we had all been in a life-threatening situation.

Finally, the house was finished. Each family had only one room, but the most important thing was that we all had separate bathrooms. Otherwise, the accommodations were primitive. The kitchen was small, but we cooked mostly on a Chinese stove in the yard. We had practically no electricity – our allotment was only one kilowatt a month. A high wooden gate with a small door for pedestrians in it closed in the courtyard and separated us from the busy street, giving us some degree of privacy. The floor throughout the house was cement. We certainly lacked luxuries, but I had had a maid, an *amah*, since our arrival in Shanghai. When the Americans began bombing Shanghai in July 1945, however, as many Chinese as were able escaped to the countryside. My *amah* was one of them, so after she left I had to take care of all the household duties myself.

~

In 1943, once we had already moved into the ghetto, Liza gave the evacuation papers that she hadn't wanted to use to a Czech doctor, Professor Příbram. Shortly before the doctor left, I needed an operation to remove my appendix and he operated on me himself, without charge, out of sheer gratitude to Liza. I had the best care possible. Professor Příbram had me admitted to the Shanghai General

Hospital, where he performed the surgery, assisted by our good friend, Dr. Grinberger. I was in the hospital for two weeks, in the care of wonderful Japanese nurses. It was very cold that winter – the temperature was only around the freezing point, but in that usually tropical climate it seemed much colder. Even in the hospital, there was no heating or electricity. After the operation, the nurses had to surround me with hot water bottles to keep me warm. My sister brought me the beautiful wool dress that I had knitted myself and I wore it throughout my recovery. I couldn't even wash myself because of the cold. When I was finally released after two weeks in bed, I couldn't straighten out. To keep myself warm, even in the house, I wore my fur coat.

The children continued to attend school while we were in Hongkew, although they had to leave the American school because it had closed after the bombing of Pearl Harbor. There was a Jewish school just across the street from the ghetto and the children were permitted to leave the ghetto to go there, but I transferred Milan to an English Catholic school instead. The Jewish school didn't have any trained instructors other than the principal – housewives and mothers took their turn at teaching. Vera had just entered Grade 1, so the teachers didn't matter quite so much for her, but Milan was older. I left him in the Catholic school as long as it was possible.

Because he was allowed to go out of the ghetto, Milan had to take on responsibility beyond his age. Sometimes I had to send him shopping and on one occasion, when I had sent him to pick something up in a restaurant, a big dog there bit him. That was a very serious issue in Shanghai – the police were called, the dog was taken for observation for rabies, and my ten-year-old boy had to go all by himself to a hospital outside of the ghetto every day for anti-rabies treatment. I had no idea where the hospital was because I couldn't leave the ghetto to go with him. Milan was supposed to get twenty-five very painful injections, but after he had had ten of them, the police told us that he could stop the treatment because the dog turned out to be healthy.

We were lucky – another dog had bitten the brother of one of our friends, Mr. Fingerut, but the dog ran away and couldn't be found for testing. His brother decided to only have twenty of the twenty-five needles and ended up dying of rabies.

It was really dangerous to live under such difficult conditions in that part of the world. There was overcrowding, malnutrition, lack of hygiene, tropical infections, and diseases like Shanghai fever, dysentery, cholera, typhus, tuberculosis and rabies. Arnold had a bout of dysentery. He fainted in bed one day and when I called the doctor, he promptly poured Arnold a large glass of whiskey and forced him to drink it. From then on, as long as we were in Shanghai, Arnold had to drink a glass of whiskey every day. After we left China, he never touched alcohol again.

I had low blood sugar, which caused frequent fainting spells, and I also got infected with liver worms. There was an epidemic of them in the ghetto – more than two thousand people were affected. Some people had terrible pain, but in others, like me, the condition caused high fevers. Years later, in Montreal, my attacks became acute again. I suffered through terrible pain for three weeks and when I went to the Montreal General Hospital, the doctor thought I was having problems with my pancreas. When he found out what it really was he was astounded – he had no idea how I could have contracted these worms, since they only existed on the Yangtze River. Once he heard my history, though, he was able to cure me with the help of some new medicine.

Life in the ghetto left much to be desired in the way of comfort, but there were many really fine people living there. One of the people that we met when we moved there was Baruch Petranka, who became Arnold's close friend. Baruch was from Poland and his wife was from Germany. Their only child, a son, was born in the ghetto near the end of the war.

Among many of our friends from Central Europe were a number of professionals. There were about 1,200 Jewish physicians in the ghetto and because there were so many they couldn't charge much for their services – their going rate for a house call was only about ten Shanghai dollars, which was very little indeed. The exchange rate in 1940 was twenty-two Shanghai dollars for one American and I could buy a hundred eggs for one US dollar. The exchange rate got progressively worse over the course of the war and by 1945 it took 395,000 Shanghai dollars to buy one American dollar. The doctors couldn't find other better-paying jobs because there was such terrible unemployment in the ghetto.

I remember visiting the home of a family named Icik whom we had befriended in Hongkew. They were from Berlin, where the man had been a prominent doctor. They had a sixteen-year-old daughter and all three of them were living in one small room that served as their kitchen, bathroom and bedroom. It was unbelievable how they lived, but not unusual – many people in the ghetto lived like that. One thing I must say, though – the Chinese in Hongkew lived far worse.

The ghetto was under the jurisdiction of the Imperial Japanese Navy's Bureau of Stateless Refugee Affairs and the two officials in charge were Kanoh Ghoya and Subinspector Okura. They had the authority to issue special passes for excursions out of the ghetto and there was always a long line of applicants – the wait usually took a large part of a day. Okura was calm, official and dangerous; Ghoya was a short man who called himself the "King of the Jews" and was prone to irrational outbursts, screaming and posturing – he was even seen slapping people in front of everyone. In spite of this overt behaviour, however, he was less dangerous than Okura, who could be quite violent.

One day the publisher of the *Shanghai Jewish News*, Mr. Ossi Levine, brought Ghoya to our house. When we got to know him better in private, we found out that Ghoya was a serious man who was fond of music and ballet. The irrational behaviour turned out to be just a cover; after this visit he gave Arnold a pass out of the ghetto that was valid for a whole month. Later, after the end of the war, Ghoya returned to the ghetto and some Jewish teenagers recognized him and began pushing him around, threatening to beat him up. Instead of fighting back, Ghoya just kept bowing and repeating, "So sorry, so sorry," until he was rescued by men who were wiser and more thoughtful.

There were war crimes trials held in Shanghai in the late winter and spring of 1946.[4] Arnold and Erna attended the proceedings and when Arnold came home, he told me that Ghoya had been able to prove that he had helped the Jews as much as he could. It turned out that he had been spying for the US and was acquitted of all charges against him. The Chinese had let us in to Shanghai and the Japanese had definitely saved our lives.

The war in Europe came to an end on May 8, 1945 – Germany had capitulated. We heard the news on my brother Vilda's short-wave radio. The Japanese authorities had issued a proclamation on November 16, 1942, forbidding us from having radios – any person who had one would be subject to the utmost penalty – but Vilda had kept his radio buried in the ground behind his house for years and only listened to it at night. That same broadcast celebrating the end of the war also included the first announcements about Jewish survivors in Europe.[5] Vilda immediately told our friend Nelly Schwartz the good news that Nelly's sister, Lotte Sulk, had survived the concentration camp in Theresienstadt and was looking for her.[6]

The victory in Europe didn't improve our situation in Shanghai, however – in fact, things got even worse when the Americans in-

---

4 The Shanghai war crimes trials of Japanese military personnel to which Anka is referring took place between February 27 and April 15, 1946.

5 After the war, the Jewish Agency set up the Search Bureau for Missing Relatives in 1945 to assist survivors in the search for family members. The bureau aired almost daily special radio broadcasts announcing names of survivors.

6 Theresienstadt was the German name for the Czech town of Terezin, sixty kilometres north of Prague, that the Nazis turned into a ghetto and a concentration camp from 1941 to 1945. For more information, see the glossary.

creased their bombing on July 17, 1945. There had been air attacks before, but we had believed that the Americans knew that 18,000 Jews were living in the Shanghai ghetto and would never hurt us. The Japanese believed that too – they probably chose Hongkew for the ghetto because they thought that our presence there would protect the large oil warehouse right across the street from our house.

Unfortunately for us, oil was essential to the Japanese war effort, so destroying the warehouse became a priority for the Americans. That was where the bombardment started on that terrible day. Surrounded by deafening explosions, we quickly pushed two tables together, placed a couch on top of them and all seven of us who were in the house at the time crowded underneath this improvised shelter. We were being subjected to what the Americans called "carpet bombing" – it was so dense that along the straight path of the bombers there was nothing left but craters.

After the bombing, Arnold got a large jar of water and left the house without telling me where he was going. I soon found out that he had walked through the ruins to find our friends Hugo, Nelly and Eva Schwartz, who lived nearby. Their house was gone, but they had survived by hiding in the basement and standing next to the chimney. Arnold brought them to our house and I moved my sister to our room to make a place for them. They were terribly dirty and Nelly was seven months pregnant – sadly, she lost her baby a few days later. In all, thirty-eight refugees and hundreds of Chinese were killed in the bombing.

Many families were now without shelter and as many as could be accommodated were moved into Czech House, now located at 41/43 Chusan Road in Hongkew. It was so crowded there that two families often had to live in one room separated by a curtain of bed sheets to give a semblance of privacy. The families lived like that until the end of the war with Japan. Everyone in the ghetto really pitched in to help each other, though. My sister, Liza, helped to cook meals for a few hundred people in Czech House.

This attack turned out to be only the first of many and the frequent bombings created a great deal of uncertainty, so, at that point, I thought it best to keep Milan closer to home and transferred him to the Jewish school inside the ghetto.

~

The unforgettable day finally came. After midnight on August 12, 1945, Baruch Petranka knocked on our gate calling, "Arnold, the war is over!" That night there was no more sleep for any of us. Everyone – those of us in the ghetto, the "native" Europeans, other refugees and the Chinese – everyone was out in the streets laughing, crying and celebrating. Allied flags were flying everywhere – there wasn't a swastika in sight.

A few days later, on August 18, the ghetto was formally dissolved, although we remained living there until we left Shanghai. The American army rescue mission arrived by air on that same day to visit the school and the prisoner of war (POW) and internment camps. Whole families had been incarcerated in internment camps since the attack on Pearl Harbor and had evidently suffered greatly – the ones we met in the market in Hongkew were just skin and bones. The Japanese had treated the Jews fairly well but were merciless in their treatment of prisoners of war and the American and British families they had put into internment camps.

The United Nations Relief and Rehabilitation Administration (UNRRA) immediately began distributing canned food, clothing and medicine. Their help was very welcome. The war was over but some people were bitterly disappointed that the Japanese authorities were still there. The victorious Allies had reportedly demanded that they stay and keep order in the huge city until the Americans could bring in the necessary personnel to take over.

On September 19, a month after the opening of the Shanghai ghetto, more than 150 American warships docked in the harbour and the city was soon swarming with young men in American military uniforms. Walking home from school, Milan met a group of soldiers who stopped him, surprised to see a blond eleven-year-old and even more surprised to find that he spoke English with an American accent. A white child in the middle of Shanghai, Milan was a reminder of home. When they found out that this handsome boy could also speak Chinese, he became their mascot. They asked him if he had a sister and when he admitted that he did, the Americans asked how old she was. Learning that Vera was only eight still didn't deter them from their quest. "You must have a young mother," they persisted, and asked to meet her. So it happened that Milan came home that day with about ten American soldiers. They all wanted steak, though, which I of course couldn't supply on such short notice, and they soon left in search of what else Shanghai had to offer.

The next day, at about ten in the morning, one soldier came to our house all alone. He was young, in his early twenties, blond and incredibly handsome. He told me that his first name was Clark and he marched into the room carrying two bags. He emptied the contents onto the table – inside were cosmetics and other goodies – anything that the GIs could buy in the post exchange (PX), a special store for American military personnel. There was also the very first pair of nylon stockings that I had ever seen. I told Clark that I didn't want any of the things that he had brought. When he sat down, I excused myself and ran to my mother's room to ask her to come and stay with me. "Just sit there and don't leave!" I told her in Czech. We talked for a little while – conversation was difficult since I didn't speak much English – but then I told him directly that my husband would be home soon and I had to cook lunch for him.

Clark was a nice, decent fellow. He came to the house again one day and brought me a plastic raincoat, another unheard-of novelty. He invited all of us to visit the American hospital ship, the USS *Repose*, which was docked in the harbour. The visit was unforgettable – it still haunts me to this day. There were padded cabins that were so small that only one person could fit inside standing up; they were for the naval officers who had gone mad during the intense battles for Okinawa and Iwo Jima.[7] Okinawa is the largest of the Ryukyu Islands off the shore of Japan and more than 12,000 Americans lost their lives in that battle, as well as almost ten times as many Japanese. At Iwo Jima, the American sailors told us that the whole island had been on fire – it was called Kazan-retto in Japanese, Sulfur Island. It's no wonder that the Americans had gone mad. The nurse explained that most of the mentally ill servicemen would eventually get better, but that about 10 per cent of them would remain incurable for the rest of their lives.

One day Milan came home late from school. I was just starting to get worried when he arrived home and happily pulled a bunch of American dollars out of his pockets. Needless to say, I was flabbergasted and asked him where he had gotten so much money. He explained that on his way from school he had met a group of American soldiers looking for a bar. He knew about one that belonged to the sister of one of our close friends. Our friend had never mentioned her – I hadn't even known that this fine gentleman had a sister, let alone one who owned a bar!

Milan recounted his story at some length, describing how they all marched into the bar, a bunch of soldiers and an eleven-year-old boy. The soldiers ordered drinks for themselves and a lemonade for Milan. I wondered where on earth my innocent little son, my pride and joy, had gotten all that information about bars. The owner approached their table and the soldiers offered her a drink, but she said she drank only milk – Milan told me that part with a derisive laugh. After a short conversation with her, the soldiers stuffed some money into Milan's pockets and told him that he could go home. Milan had

---

7 The battles of Iwo Jima (February-March 1945) and Okinawa (April-June 1945) were American military offensives to capture strategic land and air bases in Japan. Both sides suffered losses in long, bloody battles, which ultimately ended in US victories.

a knowing smirk on his face when he told me how his escapade had ended. I didn't like that smile at all, but he had developed a relationship with the American military and they were very fond of him.

By this time it was getting close to Christmas and Milan got an invitation to have Christmas dinner on one of the ships. The Shore Patrol would pick him up on Christmas morning, drive him to the ship in a Jeep and bring him back by five. When it got to be way past five and was getting very dark and Milan still wasn't home, I frantically went to the telephone booth and called the Shore Patrol – I don't even remember how I found their number, but I did. I explained to the kind man at the other end of the line that my son was on a ship and was supposed to have been home by five, but he hadn't come back. The man promised that he would look into it and call me back as soon as he knew something. I stood there waiting beside the telephone. Finally it rang and the man on the other end told me not to worry, that my son was safe, but that the motorboat that transports soldiers from ship to shore was out of order. They were working on it and as soon as it was repaired they would bring my boy home.

Milan got home just before midnight, very tired, but happy and much impressed. There was so much that he wanted to tell us. He had had lunch on one ship but afterward had been taken to many others. It seems that everybody in the American military wanted to borrow the smart and endearing eleven-year-old who spoke English like an American. When he got up the next morning, I had a chance to find out more of the details of his adventure. "How was the dinner?" I asked him. "Did you have a carp?" That was the Czech tradition on Christmas. "What carp?!" said Milan with disdain. "We had turkey!" He told me that there had been butter on the table and he showed me how big a piece of butter it was. In wonder, he went on to tell me that he had been allowed to take as much of it as he wanted. Butter was expensive in Shanghai and for years now he had only had pork lard on his bread.

He had also brought us home a letter from the American commander of one of the ships, who happened to be Jewish, offering to take Milan to America and arrange the best education for him that money could buy. Perhaps I should have accepted his offer, but how could I agree to send my child across the Atlantic alone. We all just wanted to go home.

The Pain of Knowing

Until the end of the war we knew nothing about the horrors that had happened in Europe. A few days after the peace was announced, I came home and told Arnold that I wanted to see a documentary film that was being shown at the Soviet consulate. Arnold looked at me with a very serious expression and said, "You must not go! Please, promise me that you won't go there!" He said that he and Vilda had already seen the film and that that was enough. That film was the first news about Auschwitz that had come to our colony. My husband was trying to shelter me from the devastating news.

I didn't go to see the documentary, so the first I heard about the terrible events in Europe was in September 1945, between Rosh Hashanah – the Jewish New Year – and Yom Kippur, when we received a letter from my cousin Karel Gross.[1] We used to be very close – his mother, Malva, and my mother were sisters – and Karel and his brother, Franta, were among the cousins who, in happier times, had had such fun at our wedding. In this devastating letter Karel described in agonizing detail what had happened to Arnold's parents in

---

1 Rosh Hashanah, the Jewish New Year, is the autumn holiday that marks the beginning of the Jewish year and ushers in the High Holy Days. Yom Kippur, the Day of Atonement, is a solemn day of fasting and repentance that comes ten days after Rosh Hashanah and marks the end of the High Holy Days.

the Treblinka concentration camp, as well as the fate of twenty-four of our closest relatives.[2] Among them was his mother, Aunt Malva, who had been in the camp at Theresienstadt until October 1944, but was then part of the last transport of people younger than sixty-five to be sent east to their deaths. Those over sixty-five were allowed to stay because "they would soon die anyway." Malva had turned sixty-two in June.

In 1943 the Red Cross had already informed my father that his only sister, my aunt Heda, and her daughter, Herta, had drowned on their way to Palestine when their ship, the SS *Patria*, sank in Haifa Bay on November 25, 1940 – 250 of the 1,900 passengers died. The ship had been stopped by a British patrol and the Haganah – the Jewish paramilitary force in British Mandate Palestine that later became the Israeli Defence Forces – had tried to disable the ship just enough so that the passengers would be allowed to disembark. They set off what was intended to be a minor explosion so that they could disembark, but they had underestimated its force and the ship capsized.[3] In the ensuing chaos, Herta's husband had managed to swim to shore and a British soldier had saved their eight-year-old daughter, Ruth.

Altogether, sixty-five of our relatives died in the Holocaust.

At that time we didn't know the term "nervous breakdown," but after reading the letter from Karel, Arnold just sat in an easy chair for two days, not moving, not speaking, not eating, not drinking, not sleeping. Alarmed, I called our friend Dr. Herbert Grinberger. He came right away and asked me to let him have a few words with Arnold in private. When he had finished talking to him, he told me to leave Arnold alone, not to offer him anything. "He is a strong man, he

---

2   The Treblinka death camp, about eighty kilometres northeast of Warsaw, was one of the facilities explicitly created to murder Jews in German-occupied Poland using poison gas. For more information, see the glossary.

3   The passengers of the SS *Patria* were being denied entry into Palestine because the British Mandate authorities considered them to be illegal immigrants.

will recover," he said. "This is his way of mourning, of sitting shiva."[4]

On the third day after Dr. Grinberger's visit, Arnold got up from the chair and said, "Tomorrow is Yom Kippur. You can do whatever you want, but I am not fasting. In all my life I never saw my mother in her underwear. The thought that in Treblinka she had to undress in front of everybody and, naked, my parents had to dig their own grave.... I no longer believe that there can possibly be a God...."

From then on, Arnold and I were finished with religious faith. We continue supporting Jewish causes but in our beliefs, we are secular.

~

We started looking for a way to leave Shanghai. It wasn't easy because hundreds of thousands of Europeans all over the world were trying to return home – we would have to wait our turn. Waiting in Shanghai was made more difficult by the climate – after more than five years we still weren't used to the heat, humidity and living conditions – and everything was worse in the ghetto. We had no electricity, so we couldn't even have a fan and, of course, there wasn't any air conditioning then.

Our wait was made even more difficult by the fact that my father was very ill in hospital – he was a heavy smoker and had developed lung cancer. On Sunday, February 3, 1946, as my mother and I sat by his bedside, he looked so sad that I said, "Daddy, cheer up. We're sure to be evacuated soon." When he asked, "But how will I get back to Prague in my condition?" I assured him, "Your two sons and Arnold will carry you." My father, being a Czech patriot, smiled and said, "Only to Cheb, only to the border! From there I will walk." Alas, my father passed away at eight o'clock the same evening. We cremated his remains and took the ashes back to Czechoslovakia with us – we couldn't leave him in a foreign land.

---

4 In Judaism, shiva is the seven-day mourning period that is observed after the funeral of a close family relation.

In the end, we had to wait almost six months after my father's death before we could leave China. On Monday, July 16, 1946, at six o'clock in the morning, my brother Vilda knocked on our window and said, "Get up! Tomorrow we are leaving Shanghai!"

An American military ship, the SS *Marine Angel*, had docked in Shanghai harbour to evacuate French citizens and had some space left and was willing to take on Czech passengers who had Czech passports. There were twenty-eight of us and ten of these were our family. We had to be on board the ship on Wednesday, July 17, at five o'clock in the afternoon. The *Marine Angel* was a military ship, not a luxury liner, but who cared! We were going home!

The voyage was long – as long as our first voyage to safety in Shanghai. After eight days at sea Vilda told us that there were stowaways aboard, three young Orthodox Jews. They were very religious and wouldn't eat anything, not even a slice of bread, because it might not be strictly kosher.[5] Arnold talked to the men, pleading with them to eat at least the soft, inside part of the bread. Somehow he managed to get a whole loaf for them, but they said that they would rather die than break the dietary rules. So we tried to find things that they would eat. Milan and Vera, along with Lidka and Rudla Winters' daughter, Eva, joined us in secretly smuggling food from the dining room to the stowaways, mostly raw vegetables, fruit and sardines.

When the ship docked in Port Said near the Suez Canal in Egypt, the stowaways told us that they wanted to disembark and travel to Palestine, so Arnold arranged for a small boat to take them ashore. The only problem was that they had to get to it by climbing down a rope. Arnold begged them to make an exception and leave their hats off, but they refused.[6] They simply wouldn't go without their hats, so,

---

5 Observant Jews follow a system of dietary rules known as kashruth that regulates what can be eaten, how food is prepared and how meat and poultry are slaughtered. For more information, see the glossary.

6 Observant Jewish men cover their heads, usually with a small skullcap, and some members of Orthodox sects also often wear a black, brimmed hat.

with the hats on their heads and no experience in rope-climbing, they tried to descend to the small craft. Two of them actually made it, but the third one fell in the water – fortunately, the skilled soldier manning the little boat managed to save him from drowning. He pulled him inside the boat and took all three of them to shore.

Unfortunately, however, the police arrested the three young men as soon as they stepped on solid ground. They were conspicuous with their black hats. We all agreed that something had to be done – we couldn't just leave them in jail. Arnold asked the captain if he could send a telegram from the ship and, with his permission, he telegraphed Baruch Petranka, who was still in Shanghai, to help the three boys in Port Said. Much later, when we were in Montreal, Baruch told us that Arnold's telegraph was the first news the community in Shanghai had had about the stowaways since they left. As soon as they received it, they contacted the Jewish community in Port Said, who paid whatever it cost to have the young men released and helped them on their way to Palestine.

From Port Said we continued on our journey to France and, after a total of thirty-one days at sea, we landed in the military port city of Toulon on the French Mediterranean coast. As soon as the gangplank was in place, some strong men came aboard the ship to help with the luggage. Painted on their backs in white were the letters P O W and we realized that they were German prisoners! As soon as I saw them I ran back downstairs – just seeing them made me feel like fainting. I had to lie down for half an hour to sort out my feelings – by now I was only too aware of what these "cultured" people had done.

When we finally disembarked, people from the International Red Cross were waiting for us, offering sleeping accommodations. My husband declined with thanks, telling them that we would leave it for others who needed their help more than we did, that we would go to a hotel.

From Toulon we took a train to Marseille, about sixty kilometres west along the Mediterranean coast, and arrived there on August 18,

1946. Arnold, Vilda and Rudla tried to find out how to get us to Paris, where we could board a Czech repatriation train bound for Prague. We were told that the train would wait for us in Paris for several days.

While we were out for a walk in Marseille the next day, we encountered a group of forty women and were astounded to hear them speaking Czech. We approached them and learned that they were former prisoners from various concentration camps who were now trying to get to Palestine. They advised us not to go back to Czechoslovakia because it was coming under the influence of Communism.[7] They were better informed than we were. We learned later that the chief rabbi in Prague had randomly married these women to forty young Jewish soldiers, members of the Jewish Brigade of the British army who were returning to their units in Palestine to be discharged because that was where they had volunteered for military service.[8] As wives of Allied soldiers, the women would be allowed to enter Palestine with their "husbands."

One of those girls was Anka Bohmova from Prostějov – I knew her well. She told me not only her own story, but also what she knew about the fate of my dearest cousin, Slavek Polak. On March 7, 1943 – President Masaryk's birthday – the SS in Auschwitz had gathered together the Czech *Häftlinge* (prisoners) and sent them to the gas chamber. Others, nearby, could hear them singing the Czech anthem as they walked to their deaths. Slavek Polak had been one of them.

---

7 The Communist Party of Czechoslovakia had been gradually building in influence since the 1920s, and following the country's liberation from the Nazis by the Soviet Union's Red Army at the end of World War II, the Party experienced a surge in popular support. An election in May 1946 resulted in Communist Party leader Klement Gottwald becoming prime minister.

8 The Jewish Brigade was a military unit of the British army, formed in 1944, that fought the Germans in Italy. Made up mainly of Jewish volunteers from British Mandate Palestine, the Jewish Brigade was stationed on the Italy-Austria border after the war. Members of the Brigade assisted refugees and learned about the atrocities committed against their people; some helped Holocaust survivors to immigrate to Palestine – which was illegal at the time.

The twenty-eight of us from Czechoslovakia who had been aboard the *Marine Angel* had to wait in Marseille for three days to get our train tickets to Paris. When we arrived at the Marseille station, however, we saw to our dismay that the train – both outside and inside – was completely covered with people. What was the use of having the number of our compartment if we couldn't get inside the train?

It was a hot day in southern France, so I was wearing blue shorts and a white blouse. Since there was no way that I could get through the crowd in the doorway to the train, I asked Arnold and my brothers to lift me up so I could climb in through the window. I got into the compartment and told the people inside to get out, that we had our places reserved. Although they only spoke French and probably didn't understand my words, I made it abundantly clear to them what I meant. They didn't care. I pushed my way back to the window and asked the men to pass me the suitcases. They handed them to me one by one and I threw them inside the compartment. Faced with such an intense bombardment, the interlopers finally left. We got Mother in next, then Lidka and her six-month-old baby, then Eva and Vera. The girls would sleep on suitcases in the compartment, as they always did during our travels at that time. The men, including Milan, stood in the corridor – Milan was one very tired twelve-year-old. I could see that he was asleep on his feet, but the corridor was so crowded that he couldn't fall down. That's how it was all the way to Paris.

When we got there, the Czech repatriation train to Prague hadn't arrived yet and we made good use of the time to see the sights. As we were walking on the Champs-Élysées speaking Czech, a stranger approached us. He told us that he was also Czech, but that he had lived in Paris for many years. He offered to show us the Paris nightlife if we were interested. We were! My mother stayed in the hotel with the children and we set out on our adventure.

Our new acquaintance took us around Paris and finally led us to a nightclub. As soon as we walked in through the door a woman approached my sister and kept touching her as she talked to her. We didn't understand what she was saying, but it was strange behaviour. When I looked around in wonder, I realized that there were only women in the club. It took a while for it to dawn on us that we were in a lesbian club. By that time it was late and the women had had enough. We decided to return to our hotel, but the men were enjoying themselves and wanted to stay a while longer. We were very independent women and declined an escort, telling the men that there was nothing to worry about – Liza, Lidka, five other women and I would all take the metro back to our hotel. In the labyrinth of the Paris underground, however, we lost our way. We rode all the way to the end of the line, then to the other end. By the time we finally arrived at the hotel, the men were already there, somewhat worried.

We left for Prague a few days later. That train was also crowded – for years after the war, all the trains remained crowded because so many people had been displaced. People everywhere were coming to terms with their situation, looking for a place to settle down and start over again. On the repatriation train, only women with children could get sleeping accommodations for the long trip back home. The going was very slow. We had to cross Germany, where the tracks were still disrupted from the Allied bombing. When we stopped in Frankfurt, the only way we could tell that we were in a station was that there were two men with whistles on the platform wearing the usual blue uniforms and red hats of European railway services.

A Czech woman who had also boarded the repatriation train in Paris had been a prisoner in the Ravensbrück concentration camp during the war.[9] When she saw that Frankfurt had been completely destroyed, she leaned out the open window and called out, "Beautiful

---

9 Ravensbrück was the largest Nazi concentration camp designed almost exclusively for women, and about 3 per cent of the camp inmates were Czech. For more information, see the glossary.

Frankfurt! God, am I happy! Do I ever wish it on you! You deserve it!" Granted, hers was not an expression of a noble spirit, but such feelings were understandable after so much injustice, suffering and hate had been unleashed on all of us.

The train stopped for meals, which were cooked in a designated car. All the passengers had to get off the train and stand in line. There were some students from Prague University on the train with us. Czech universities had been closed after student demonstrations in the fall of 1939 and many of the students had been carted off to concentration camps or had been taken to serve as slave labour in German factories. When some of the students saw me in my navy blue shorts and white top they must have thought that I was far younger than I was – they were appalled that I had taken one of the prized places in a sleeping car. "You have some nerve," they told me. "Only women with children are supposed to be in the sleeping car!" I told them that I did have children, but they didn't believe me and dismissed me with disgust. Still wanting to defend myself, I insisted that I was indeed married with two children. If they wanted to see my children, I told them, they could come to our car. I'm not sure that I ever managed to convince them that I wasn't still a student.

～

We arrived in Prague at noon on September 1, 1946. Helena Ganzova – now Grossova– was waiting for us at the station with her brother-in-law and my cousin, Karel Gross, the only member of my family who had survived the concentration camps. A German friend – the woman whose brother had accompanied my parents and Liza to Berlin on their way to Shanghai – had saved Karel's life by sending him parcels of food while he was in Theresienstadt. I never heard what happened to her brother – as a German soldier, he might have lost his life during the war. I do know that after liberation his sister and their parents were rounded up with other Germans and taken to the trade fair, or exhibition, palace on Veletržní třída (Veletržní

Road), the same place where Jewish families had had to spend the night before they were taken to Theresienstadt.

We heard that in Prague, the Nazis had been "clever" in dealing with their defenseless captives – they had been careful not to openly mistreat them. Instead, they had marched them to the train station and loaded them into cattle cars in the dark of the night. In contrast, the post-war Czech guards – most of them former Czech soldiers – were angry rather than clever. Perhaps they wanted the Germans to know what it felt like to be on the receiving end of their cruelty. Karel's German friend later described terrible scenes that she had witnessed after being rounded up – the beatings were so ferocious that the floor and walls were splattered with blood. Karel found out where she was and managed to get her and her parents out of there. We later heard that they married and settled in Chicago. We also learned that unfortunately, after her terrible post-war experience, this remarkable woman completely lost the regard she used to have for humanity.

Helena Grossova had been Liza's schoolmate and best friend; she was also one of the social work students who had secretly graduated with Liza in 1939. After we left for China, she met our cousin Franta Gross (Karel's brother) and in those difficult times of great oppression, the two young people had gotten married. Their happiness didn't last long – they were taken to Theresienstadt and eventually put on a transport to the East.[10] They both managed to survive in Auschwitz, but both suffered terribly there and, later, in several different concentration camps.

Toward the end of the war, when the front was already on German occupied soil, Hitler ordered the evacuation, on foot if necessary, of

---

10 Jews in Theresienstadt – and in other Nazi concentration and transit camps – were routinely told that they were going to be "resettled in the East," but instead were deported to death camps and forced labour camps in German-occupied Eastern Europe.

concentration camp inmates.[11] None of them were provided with even the barest essentials for survival. Helena's husband – Franta – had been on one such "death march" from Mauthausen concentration camp when the Americans liberated him.[12] They took him to a hospital in Pilsen, in western Bohemia about ninety kilometres west of Prague, where they fed him only champagne, one spoonful at a time. He was too weak to tolerate any other food. His brother, Karel, found him there and insisted on taking him to Prague. There, two weeks after liberation, Franta Gross died. Helena was now a widow.

Helena later told us her own story of being on another death march. Weak and in pain, with a badly infected knee, just as she knew that she wouldn't be able to walk any farther, a female guard had inadvertently saved her life by kicking Helena's infected knee so hard that the pus flew right into the guard's face. Furious, she had beaten Helena, but the knee, drained of its infection, had healed.

When we arrived in Prague, Helena took my mother and my sister to her small apartment. Erna and his wife, Hilda, were invited to stay with Hilda's uncle, Mr. Müller, her father's brother. He was married to a Christian woman and she had helped him to survive the war. Arnold, the children and I had to go to a hotel. We had no home – no apartment, no house, no business – nothing. We stayed at a hotel on Na Poříčí, one of Prague's main avenues.

Early on our first morning back in Prague, I went out, eager to see my hometown again. A few steps from the hotel, quite unexpectedly, I ran into my former schoolmate Mana Langova, who recognized me right away. "You're alive!" she exclaimed in surprise. "Why shouldn't

---

11 Once Germany's defeat in the war was imminent, Heinrich Himmler ordered camp inmates to be moved in forced marches toward the German interior and all traces of the concentration camps to be covered up by burning the evidence of the camps and gas chambers.

12 The Mauthausen concentration camp, located about twenty kilometres east of the Austrian city of Linz, was known as one of the harshest labour camps established by the Nazis. For more information, see the glossary.

I be?" I replied. There was something in her tone that had made me feel defensive. "Oh, well," she continued, "I guess it's because you were different – you were more like one of us. You used to speak Czech."

Her comment hit me like a slap in the face – that was my welcome home. It stirred up a wave of anger and painful disappointment in me. What did her explanation mean? Is it possible that so much could have changed here in such a short time? That after all the patriotism in Shanghai, after the longing for home, was it possible that I didn't belong here any more? I pounced on Mana in fury. I shook her by the neck and called her a bitch. Then, crying bitterly, I ran upstairs to our room. Arnold was alarmed and asked me what had happened. I cried and cried and when I stopped, I pleaded with him to let us all leave Prague right away.

In his usual calm manner, Arnold said that six years ago we had left everything as it stood – now he wanted to find out more about the fate of our friends and relatives. Since he was in charge of our finances, he also needed to see whether there was any part of our family fortune left. I wasn't thinking about possessions, I was crying for my beloved homeland, for the relatives that I would never see again, for our lost years. Even though I consciously knew better, deep down I still harboured the unreasonable expectation that after all the suffering, after the worldwide upheaval, that Prague would have somehow stayed the same.

I began looking into whether anything of the old Prague had survived the war. It all seemed so strange now. The first one of my best friends that I found was Marta Mautnerova, whose married name was now Pekova. She and her husband were back living in their prewar apartment – some of the first returnees from the concentration camps had been able to get their homes back, something that was no longer possible for those of us who came back later. Marta told me that her own furniture was still in the apartment, but that when she opened the wardrobe there was a German uniform with the SS insignia hanging inside it.

Marta also told me something about what life had been like in Prague after we left. Her husband, Karel Peka, had been among the first group taken to Theresienstadt in November 1941. After the village had been cleared of the local Czech inhabitants, he and the other men were sent there to prepare the area for the influx of inmates that would soon be arriving. Marta and her daughter, Alenka, had been sent there some months later, in 1942. They had all survived in Theresienstadt by a series of miracles. At one point, they had been on the list for an eastbound transport that was scheduled to leave the next morning. For some unknown reason, one of the SS guards, a man originally from Sudeten who was known to be constantly intoxicated, had entered the isolated compound before the transport left and taken them out. That was unheard of! Perhaps the man drank to block out what was happening around him, and tried to save at least some of the Jewish prisoners. This particular SS guard was exonerated at one of the war crimes trials in Prague after the war and Karel Peka was one of the eight people who had testified on his behalf.

When children arrived in Theresienstadt, they were supposed to be put in the orphanage, but Marta had somehow managed to keep her six-year-old daughter with her. They slept together on the same plank and, during the day, while her mother was working, Alenka had to stay where they slept. She was there on the day that all children from the orphanage were transported to the east and never seen or heard from again. Alenka was one of the few children who survived the camp.

Marta recounted events of suffering and extreme depravity alongside stories of selflessness and heroism. The story of the renowned Jewish swim team from the Hagibor Jewish sports club in Prague is quite unforgettable. The Czech gendarmes guarding the outside of the camp would sometimes carry letters for the inmates and mail them outside the guarded perimeter of Theresienstadt. They did that at the utmost personal risk since it was Nazi policy to keep their activities strictly secret – no one was to know what was happening behind the high walls and barbed wire fences of their concentration camps.

Sometime in 1942, however, one of the gendarmes was caught. There was a big uproar, during which all the inmates were forced out to a large open space and ordered to admit who else was sending letters. No one came forward. Finally they were all told that unless somebody confessed, every tenth prisoner would be executed. There were hundreds of prisoners standing there. Among them were the members of the renowned Jewish Hagibor swim team, some of the best swimmers in Europe. In order to save so many others, these boys stepped forward and were executed the same evening. Marta didn't know anything about what had happened to the gendarme, though.

The counting of the camp inmates was always a terrible event. Marta recalled one particular experience in which all the inmates, without exception, including the old people and children, were sent out into a cold, pouring rain and left standing there all day without food. Some had collapsed and died in the oozing mud and human waste. They were finally dismissed to return to their bunks late in the evening, long after dark. As a result of her experiences, Marta became an ardent Communist after the war, sincerely believing in the Communist mission of building a just society.

Marta also knew that the woman who had taught me and Liza knitting had been in Theresienstadt, working at sorting the contents of the suitcases that new arrivals had to leave on the platform when they got off of the train. When the war was over, she had filled two suitcases with men's clothing, one for her husband and one for her son. Since she was one of the early returnees to Prague after the liberation, she was able to get her apartment back and there she waited for her family to return. Then she learned that her husband and son had been sent on a death march during the concentration camp evacuations near the end of the war. By the time their wretched group of prisoners had reached the vicinity of Ostrava, in northeastern Moravia near the Polish and Slovak borders, her son and husband were too weak to continue and the frantic guards, in a headlong flight before the advancing Soviet army, had shot and killed them. When she heard the news, that good woman committed suicide by throwing herself out of the window of her fourth floor apartment.

We stayed in the hotel for several weeks, until a trade fair and the resulting shortage of hotel rooms made the rates go up. Living in a hotel was altogether inconvenient anyway – food was still rationed and we had to eat breakfast, lunch and dinner at restaurants, which wasn't good for the children. It was time for me to look for an apartment. After much searching I found a flat with a beautiful balcony in the Letná district, on Ovenecká Street, that belonged to a divorcée, a hairdresser named Mrs. Novakova. When I entered the place, she pointed to the carpet and said, "This is a real Persian carpet, do you like it?" I had a bad feeling about that – if she had really bought the carpet herself, she would have known that it wasn't Persian, it was Chinese.

I took the apartment just the same, as there was no choice. The furniture was beautiful, but the rent was high. I found out later that her rent was 2,500 korun a year, but she was charging us the same amount for a month. As soon as we moved in I called my former maid, Andulka. She was married now, and her family name was Kostelecky. She agreed to come every morning at eight and stay with us until about seven. On the first day, when Andulka pulled the furniture away from the wall to clean the floor, she noticed that the back of every piece was marked in chalk with a Jewish name: Kohn and Wiener and.... During the deportations, when the Jewish families were taken to Theresienstadt, the furnishings from their homes were carted off to warehouses where anyone could buy it – there was a lot of it and the prices were low. I didn't recognize any of the pieces and none were marked with the names Voticky or Kanturek, which would have been far too much of a coincidence.

We lived in that apartment for about a year and we enrolled our children in school right away. They could speak Czech, but they didn't know any grammar. To remedy that, they were accepted into lower grades, to be promoted later as their skills increased. I also went to the Jewish Town Hall, the community centre, and spoke to the rabbi about changing our religion back to Jewish.

I was reminded all too often that this was not the Prague I used to know, the Prague to which we had longed to return. There was still a post-war shortage of food and we all spent a lot of time standing in lines. Imported fruit such as oranges only came in occasionally and one day, as I stood in line for them, an ugly woman turned to me and said, "You see, we get only one orange per person, but Jews get three!" "That's not true," I retorted. I didn't know that right after the war, the people who came back from the concentration camps got double rations for six weeks. That small generosity caused envy, even hostility, among some people. Another woman in line spoke up and said, "It's true, they do get three oranges!" A third woman interrupted this brilliant conversation by attacking me personally; "Why do you take their side? What do you have in common with them?"

At this point I could have said, "I'm Jewish and as you can see, I only have one orange, like everybody else," but I was hurt and instead of answering I left the orange there, ran home and told Arnold, "It's time to leave!" I was very upset. I had the same education, spoke the same language and had been brought up to be a patriot. My father used to say, "You are Czech in nationality and Jewish in religion."

Soon after we moved from the hotel to the furnished flat, I tried to find our former maid, Fanda. I knew that her parents had lived in a modest little house by the Elbe River, but I had heard that she was now living near where the old synagogue used to be. Following my hazy memories, I found it. The building was dilapidated and was now being used as a warehouse. Equally in disrepair, with bare bricks showing underneath the falling plaster, was the house next door where the *shames* – the synagogue caretaker – used to live. I asked a woman who appeared at the entrance where I could find Mrs. Nebeska. The woman gave me a long, sad look and finally said, quietly and reproachfully, "Anynko, don't you recognize me?"

Fanda had aged beyond her years. She used to be tall and slim, but this woman was stout and careworn. She was a widow now – her husband had died during the war, as had her daughter. Her son, who was born in 1921, lived in Brno. The family must have lived through hard times. Even now, Fanda's home was a very modest one room with a brick floor. I visited her a few times while we were still in Prague.

We all were trying to pick up the pieces of our lives and reconcile ourselves with our losses. Two years after the war, we were still spending much of our time looking for friends and family members who might have survived. Our cousin Karel Gross found by chance one of his childhood friends, Franta Vilim from Pardubice. In better times Karel and Liza had played tennis with Franta whenever they visited our Aunt Malva. So much had happened since then, so many years had passed.

Franta had been in the Allied army in England, but when Svoboda's army was being founded in the Soviet Union, they had needed officers right away.[13] The Soviet government had turned to the Czechoslovak government-in-exile in London, who took on the task of selecting the best officer material from among the Czechoslovak volunteers for them. Some commander had come up with the idea that the fastest way to do this would be to invite the likely candidates to dinner. Those who had the best table manners would then be sent to the Soviet Union.

One of the men who had been picked to go to the Soviet Union was Franta, Liza and Karel's childhood friend, who also happened to be serving with the unit that liberated Auschwitz. When he entered the compound he saw with astonishment someone he recognized walking toward him. It was Thein, the son of his cousin from Pardubice! Like all the prisoners, the young man was just skin and

---

13 General Ludvík Svoboda was commander of the Czechoslovak army, comprised of troops of varying nationalities, of which 6 per cent were Jews. In 1943–1944, his unit fought against the Germans on the eastern front alongside the Soviet Red Army and liberated part of Czechoslovakia in the 1944 Battle for the Dukla Pass.

bones, a walking skeleton wearing the striped rags of concentration camp inmates. Vilim got him a Soviet military uniform and, as the front advanced, took him all the way to Prague.

Franta also brought back from Auschwitz Dr. Ganza, Helena's uncle, her father's brother. We met him after our return from China and he told us about the last days of my brother-in-law, Armin Knopfelmacher. When the Americans bombed the camp's industrial area in August 1944, Armin, a dentist, had been working in a cellar, ordered to remove gold fillings from the teeth of dead people.[14] He didn't hear the alarm when it sounded. He walked out in the middle of the bombardment and was wounded in the back. When Dr. Ganza visited him in the infirmary, Armin had been in terrible pain. Desperate for morphine, he asked Dr. Ganza to remove Armin's own gold dental work and exchange it with an SS officer for the painkilling drugs. Dr. Ganza didn't have his implements with him, but he promised to come back the next day. By the time he returned, however, Armin's bed was empty – he was dead.

Our carefree days in Pardubice seemed like memories from some previous life. My sister had been an accomplished, beautiful and courageous twenty-two-year-old when she and my parents had left for China seven years ago. Now, when Franta and Liza finally found each other again, Franta was thirty-two and Liza was almost thirty. They decided to get married and had a short, simple wedding that was a far cry from the one Arnold and I had had back in 1933. Within a year, their daughter, Helenka, was born in Prague; their twins, a son, Tomy, and a daughter, Kaca, were born seven years later, in May 1954, in Montreal.

---

14 Between August and September 1944, the US bombed German oil refineries within range of the Auschwitz main camp. On August 20, 1944, US fighter planes bombed Buna, the synthetic-oil and rubber plant at Monowitz-Auschwitz III, which housed more than 10,000 slave-labour prisoners and was located five kilometres from the main camp.

Fleeing Yet Again

Near the end of February 1948, the Communists staged a coup and took over Czechoslovakia.[1] We were on a ski holiday at the time in Riesengebirge – the Krkonoše or Giant Mountains in northern Bohemia near the Polish border – at a place called Černá Hora. There was a nice hotel that, incidentally, had belonged to Hermann Goering during the Nazi regime.[2] About two weeks after the coup, after lunch on a warm, sunny day while we were still in Riesengebirge, I was sitting in the sun in one of the reclining chairs, surrounded by a number of other guests who were doing the same thing. All of a sudden I saw Arnold running toward us and commented to the man sitting next to me that something serious must have happened – my husband was a dignified man and the only time I ever saw him running was when he was playing soccer.

When he reached me Arnold whispered in my ear, "Jan Masaryk is dead." Jan Masaryk was the son of the first president of Czechoslovakia and minister of foreign affairs in the post-war government and a

---

1 In February 1948, under the leadership of Klement Gottwald, the Communist Party of Czechoslovakia staged a non-violent coup that effectively ended democratic governance in Czechoslovakia until 1990.

2 Hermann Goering was Hitler's designated successor and commander-in-chief of the Luftwaffe (German air force).

staunch anti-communist. He had apparently fallen out of a window at his residence. We had no way of knowing whether he committed suicide or was pushed, but, in any case, there's no doubt that his death was connected to the political developments in the country.[3]

I wanted to go back to Prague right away, but Arnold wanted me to stay and enjoy my vacation as best I could. We returned to Prague a week later and found that many of our friends had already left, including Franta Popper, and his beautiful and elegant wife, Heda. We had met them in Shanghai. My gynecologist, Dr. Steinbach, had also left.

What were we to do now? The children were going to school as usual, but we were very unsettled by the events that were unfolding around us. We would sometimes take a nap after lunch for no other reason than to escape the indecision and uncertainty. That's how depressed we were. We had opened a jewellery store in Carlsbad (Karlovy Vary in Czech) when we came back from China – Erna had moved there to run it. Arnold had promised his friend in Prague that he would not ask for the return of the Prague store. One day I asked Arnold to call the Carlsbad store and ask our saleswoman, Louise, whether she could help us get out of the country – her sister worked as a nanny for the Canadian military attaché. Arnold made the call right away and half an hour later, Louise's sister telephoned us and told us to come to Rytířská Street at seven o'clock that evening and bring our passports – we would be meeting with Mr. Irwin, the Canadian passport officer.

We walked down the hill to where my sister and her husband lived in Letná. Without any preamble, I told Franta that we had a chance to get visas to immigrate to Canada, and that he should go downtown

---

3   The investigation into Jan Masaryk's death was re-opened several times, in 1968, 1993 and 2002. The final verdict was that he was indeed murdered, although the new evidence about his death did not lead to any prosecutions. For more information, see the glossary.

with Arnold to meet the Canadian official. Franta's English was better than my husband's since he had been in the Czechoslovak army in England during the war. But my brother-in-law replied, "We aren't going anywhere, we're comfortable here. My wife is working, I'm working…. We can live under any government." But I was adamant, telling him fiercely, "We have lost enough relatives! The family stays together and where I go my sister goes. You go with Arnold!" In the end he did.

Mr. Irwin told them to come see him at the Canadian consulate the next morning. This time, Arnold went alone. Mr. Irwin was only willing to offer him one immigration visa – for himself. He explained that once Arnold was already in Canada, he could sponsor his wife and children. He obviously didn't realize how serious the situation in Czechoslovakia really was. Arnold thanked him and said that he couldn't accept just the one visa and told him that many men had done the same thing at the beginning of the war and had never seen their families again. If Mr. Irwin gave him a visa, it would have to be for the whole family. In the end, Mr. Irwin gave Arnold eighteen visitor visas – enough for our whole family and for my husband's cousins. He told us that a year after we got to Canada, we would be able to apply for immigration visas.

We were still living in the flat rented from Mrs. Novakova. One day the janitor came to tell me that the apartment above ours had become vacant and urged me to apply for it right away. The very next day, however, he came back to tell me that it had been given to a German Communist and suggested that I complain. If I did, he said that he and the other tenants would support me. I thanked him and told him that it didn't matter – we would be leaving soon for Canada. Our personal belongings were spread out on the living room floor while we prepared to have them cleared through customs. Every item had to be duly counted – how many pieces of clothing, how many handkerchiefs – listed on paper signed by witnesses and stamped by customs. Our maid, my mother and my cousin all had to confirm that the clothes were used. We ended up having to pay 99,268 Czech korun in customs duties.

We already had transit visas to travel through England, but we now had to make the rounds of the various ministries to apply for exit visas. The main problem was the revenue department, where we had to get permission to take our personal belongings out of the country and pay all of our dues. The person in charge was a lawyer named Mr. Smrcka and every day for a whole month he would invite me to come to his office – he "only" wanted me to spend a weekend with him in his country house. "What would I do with the children?" I asked him. "Your husband will take care of them," he replied calmly.

I never told Arnold about Smrcka's request. He was a powerful man; we needed him and he knew it. We had tickets to Montreal and our route there was very roundabout. We would be travelling by train to England and then by ship, on the SS *Britannica*, all the way to New York. Our itemized list of personal belongings had already been cleared and on Friday, June 5, I had to go back to Mr. Smrcka's office. He still wouldn't give me the stamps. Instead, he promised that if I came back on Monday, he would give them to me then. I was so upset that I forgot our passports on his desk. I took a taxi home and when I got there, Arnold was watching for me out the window. As I got out of the car, I told him what had happened with the passports and he said, "You must go back and fetch them."

So I got into the taxi and back I went. But by the time I got there, the office was closed, even though it was only two o'clock on a Friday afternoon. The cleaner gave me Mr. Smrcka's address and I asked the taxi driver to take me there. I asked him to wait five minutes for me and, if I wasn't out by then, to come and get me. Mr. Smrcka opened the door and I shouted at him, "Where are my passports!" "Mrs. Voticky," he answered in a soothing tone, "they're in my desk. I'll give them to you on Monday with the stamps."

We left Prague on June 10, 1948. The four of us, along with Liza, her husband, Franta, their baby and my mother, were all leaving

Czechoslovakia once again. Vilda had decided not to come with us because he was a lawyer and wanted to have a chance to practice his profession – he wouldn't be able to do that very easily in Canada. Erna and Hilda were staying behind to run the store in Carlsbad. They now had two daughters – Hilda had been pregnant when we left Shanghai and Jana was born in Prague in 1947.

Emigrants Once More

We travelled to England via Belgium. We weren't supposed to stop off anywhere until we were ready to board the ship to Canada, but we had important business to do in Brussels – for the last two years, Arnold had been transferring valuables through a Polish couple who had been living in Belgium for some time. The couple often travelled to Prague and Arnold always gave the woman a lot of jewellery to wear and American currency that, as foreigners, they could take across the border without any difficulty. Arnold had paid them two hundred dollars per trip for this service – at that time it was a lot of money. Now, we were in Belgium to pick it all up. When we arrived in Brussels by train at noon, the couple was waiting for us at the station. They took us to their apartment and in their bedroom we saw most of what they had brought through for us laid out on the bed.

We had met the Polish couple through a Jewish Slovak man we had originally met in Shanghai who was now in Belgium as well. This man – I don't remember his name (actually, I don't want to remember his name) – had taken a lot of our jewellery to a pawnshop in a town near the Dutch border and pawned it for 600 US dollars on our behalf because we needed the cash. The Slovak man now demanded that we pay him the whole $600 as a commission for recommending the Polish couple. We were in a quandary – we didn't want to give him the only US cash we had with us – but we had to settle the matter quickly because we were taking a terrible risk in staying in Belgium without the proper papers. The rest of our US dollars were already in America – when Vilda had gotten the money out of the bank in Switzerland before the war, he had sent it in US dollars to a trusted friend in the United States, Mr. Hoffman, for safekeeping. Once we had agreed to pay the man, Arnold went with him to redeem the jewellery – the only way that we could raise the necessary funds to redeem the pawned gold was to sell a few pieces in a hurry, including a valuable platinum bracelet that was so heavy it was really for decoration.

Those were tense hours! We were desperate, waiting in that apartment for Arnold in a foreign country without a visa, in danger of being sent back to Communist Czechoslovakia, not even knowing what other surprises might be in store for us. I will always remember my mother sitting on a wooden chair in the kitchen, not moving, like a piece of furniture. I, on the other hand, was pacing. The children were very quiet. The hours were passing and it was getting dark. Finally, late in the evening – it must have been nine o'clock or even later – the door opened. As soon as the Slovak man stepped inside, I confronted him, asking, "What have you done with my husband?" Then I saw Arnold follow him into the kitchen. He said to me, "Leave him alone, we can't start any trouble – we're in this country illegally." The man left with the commission he had extorted from us. The matter of a commission had never been discussed – had the man made his expectations clear to us ahead of time, Arnold would have been prepared for it. We thanked the Polish couple for their help and hospitality and they took us to the hotel they had booked for us. The next day, at noon, we were back at the railway station to board the same train to England that we had gotten off exactly twenty-four hours earlier, which now took us to the coast to a boat to cross the English Channel.

When the boat across the English Channel arrived in Southampton, the train to London was already waiting. We were the last to leave the boat, but Arnold wanted to make sure that the customs official made an itemized list of everything we had with us. He was thinking ahead. He realized that when we left England, we might need proof that we had brought the jewellery into the country with us, that we hadn't acquired it in England. It was all very confusing because every country had a different set of rules. Arnold had packed all the jewellery in a scarf and the customs official started to go through it and write the description of a few of the pieces. The train was waiting, however, and the official still had a heavy bundle before him, so he summed it all up in the phrase, "...and a lot of other jewellery." So much for playing it safe and having an itemized document!

We got on the train to London and when we arrived, we went to a hotel. To our surprise, sitting in the reception area, we found Hugo and Nelly Schwartz with their child. Franta and Heda Popper were also there, as well as the Gottwalds with their two children – all people we had known in Shanghai.

The Gottwalds had unfortunately had a hard time in England. Their name was the same as that of the current Communist president of Czechoslovakia, so they had to report to the police every day. To make matters worse, Mrs. Gottwald was Russian. The Cold War was beginning and, in those circumstances of tension between the Soviet Union and the West, that seemed suspicious indeed.

We stayed in London for about a week. My mother's brother, Richard Kohn, was living there and during our stay at the hotel, we also ran into my sister's former boyfriend, Karel Matcha. I asked him whether he was also emigrating, but he answered self-righteously, "No, madam, I am too much of a patriot. I love my native land!" "Mazel tov (Good luck)," I thought. Years later, when my sister visited Czechoslovakia, she invited him out to lunch for old time's sake. He couldn't afford to pay.

Karel Matcha was also in possession of a precious Dutch painting that Arnold and I had received as a wedding present. When I was leaving for Shanghai, Liza had left it in his care until our return and I had forgotten all about it. Years later, when we were in Canada, an acquaintance of ours, Eva Ehrman, who had known Matcha in Prague, mentioned to me that he had a beautiful 1835 Dutch painting in his living room. As soon as I heard about it, I remembered that the painting belonged to me.

My sister promptly wrote a letter to Karel asking him to return the painting, but he replied that he couldn't because after all those years, he had gotten used to having it hanging in his apartment. When I went back to Prague in 1963, I told the story to my cousin Jirka Polak. He certainly wasn't leaving the decision up to Karel Matcha – he had no patience for the excuse that he was keeping the painting because he was "used to" it. Jirka had been an officer in the Czechoslovakian army in England during the war and now had two sons. The three of them went to Karel's place and demanded the return of the painting. He took it off of the wall right away and gave it to them. I brought it back with me to Montreal.

I have another story about Jirka Polak. He was a Communist idealist who had fought in the West and sincerely believed in justice and equality for all. When he returned to Prague, still wearing the uniform of the Western allies, he found himself among the Germans who had been rounded up in the palace on Veletržní třída. A German woman approached him and pleaded with him to get some medication that she needed for her child. Jirka refused. In those days, after the concentration camps were liberated and the Nazi crimes had come to light, nearly everyone hated all Germans indiscriminately. The woman kept begging Jirka for help – after all, her child's life depended on it. In desperation she told Jirka that she was from Sudeten, where she had buried a hoard of gold. She promised to give him a map to the treasure if he would only get the medication for her daughter. Jirka kept brushing her off, but in the end he did go to the drugstore and get the medication. The woman gave him the map.

In the middle of the post-war chaos, Jirka took the map to Liberec – in the northern Bohemian region near the Polish border, about one hundred kilometres northeast of Prague – where, in the company of several policemen, he followed the directions and found the treasure. To his surprise, the policemen began happily dividing the gold amongst themselves. Astounded, Jirka objected. What were they doing? The gold belonged to the state – after all, the treasury was empty after the war. The policemen just laughed and told him not to worry, that he would get his share, too. That was where Jirka's idealism came to an end. For this he had volunteered in the army? For this he had fought? On that day, he was finished with the Communist Party.

~

From London we sailed to New York on the SS *Britannica*. We stayed there for a few days – Arnold's brother Franta and his wife, Vlasta, were living there and we had a lot to catch up on.

Franta and Vlasta had been lucky. Some time before the Nazis occupied what remained of Czechoslovakia, Franta and his wife had been on holiday in the United States. They had returned to Prague but when the occupation began in 1939 their tourist visas were still valid, so they immediately left again for the United States. By the time their ship reached New York, however, their visas had expired and they had had to spend some time detained on Ellis Island before they were permitted to land.[1] They had followed the events in Europe intensely all through the war. Now they sadly recounted that the Gestapo had picked up Vlasta's brother, Pepik Kolinsky, in Prague in 1943 just for sitting on a park bench across from the Wilson Station. They later learned that he had been executed.

There were quite a few letters waiting for us when we arrived in New York. Our friend Baruch Petranka and other people we had

---

1   The US federal immigration office on Ellis Island in New York Harbor was the main receiving station for European immigrants between 1892 and 1924. After 1924, and until 1954, refugees or displaced persons were processed in the facility.

known in Shanghai were now living in Montreal and Baruch had already spread the news that we were on our way. We had to tell him, though, that our planned destination was Toronto, where we had already agreed to meet our friends the Pachls. Arnold and Mr. Pachl had been schoolmates and after we returned from China, we had befriended his family. Their daughter, Jana, and Vera were the same age and had both taken ballet lessons in the New German Theatre in Prague – now known as the Prague State Opera.

In his letter, Baruch wrote that our Shanghai friends would like us to come to Montreal – on that basis, Arnold bought new tickets without even knowing if we could get a refund for our unused tickets to Toronto. As it turned out, the tickets were nonrefundable, which Arnold definitely regretted since they had cost a significant sum in our situation. Still, we had already lost so much that it didn't seem to matter. We felt extremely lucky to have come out of the war alive. Our family fortune was the least of our losses. We had lost so many of our relatives and friends, as well as much of the status, prestige and reputation that we and our parents had worked so hard to earn. Arnold and I were now in our late thirties; we were a family with two children, trying to establish ourselves all over again in a foreign land.

Safe and Free

When we arrived in Montreal on July 1, 1948, Baruch Petranka was waiting for us at Windsor Station. He took us to a small hotel where he had reserved two rooms, one for our family and one for Mother. The hotel was on Dorchester Street, later renamed René Lévesque. The hotel isn't there any more – in its place now stands the much larger Hotel Sheraton. We began looking for a place to settle, but it wasn't easy because even three years after the war there were still housing shortages. All the soldiers returning home from overseas were getting married and starting families, and there were many immigrants like us. We finally found an apartment in a humble but brand-new building on Ridgevale Avenue – later renamed St. Kevin Avenue – in an area of town known as Côte-des-Neiges.

We soon realized that more and more people in the current wave of refugees arriving from Communist Czechoslovakia were coming to live in that area – they were coming in droves. It seemed as if a new two-story tenement house was going up very month – for the next two years Ridgevale Avenue became the street of the Czechs.

My brother Erna and his family arrived a few weeks later, though their route was very different. The first that we heard of their arrival was the news that Erna, his wife, Hilda, and their daughters Eva and Jana were all in jail in Halifax! A customer from Canada at our jewellery store in Carlsbad had told Erna that if he ever wanted to immigrate to Canada, he would sponsor him. It turned out, however, that this customer, who had been living in Montreal for thirty years, had never taken Canadian citizenship. Only Canadian citizens could sponsor immigrants, so the man couldn't legally bring Erna and his family into the country; they were arrested upon entry. Arnold immediately took a train to Halifax and called his brother in New York to send $6,000 to get Erna and his family out of jail. That was the amount of money they needed to have to show that they were able to support themselves and be allowed into the country.

We all settled into our new life in Canada. Within two years of our decision to move to Montreal, all of the people we had known from Shanghai had left to make their homes in Toronto or farther west in Canada, or in the United States. Nonetheless, we decided to stay in Montreal and were very glad to have come to the end of our peregrinations.

Our friend Helena Grossova was still living in Prague and we wanted her to join us in Montreal, but we couldn't sponsor her because we were still just immigrants ourselves in 1950 – we didn't have Canadian citizenship yet. Liza, Franta and Helenka had joined us in Montreal by this time – they had stayed in Holland for a little while and then flown to New York before coming to Canada. After she arrived, my sister managed to get two elderly ladies to sponsor Helena to come to Montreal as a domestic servant. According to their agreement, she would have to work for them for a year. They were pleased to have her and no wonder! Aside from all her other attributes, Helena was an excellent cook. After her year was up, she got a job as a social worker. With all of the post-war immigrants coming to Canada, hospitals were looking for trained social workers who knew many languages. By the mid-1970s, Helena was in charge of the department of social work at St. Mary's Hospital.

As I've mentioned, Helena had been widowed after her brief marriage to our cousin Franta. One day, when Arnold went to see a business acquaintance in Toronto – a Czech fellow named Leo Polak – he found that the man's wife had recently died. They had a six-year-old son and the household was in a sad state, so he urged the man to get married again as soon as possible. The boy needed a mother and Arnold immediately thought of Helena. Mr. Polak came to Montreal and Helena agreed to marry him. Although we had encouraged her at first, I found her sudden decision startling. I told her that I had my doubts, but she argued that she had been a widow for a long time and was now in her mid-thirties – this might be her last chance to marry again. Helena was a beautiful woman who had had much misfortune in her life.

The marriage unfortunately didn't end up being a happy one, but Helena was an excellent mother to the boy. He was a slow learner and had to repeat Grade 1, but she helped him with his studies. He worked hard all the way through university and became a chemist. The boy was very fond of his stepmother and even his father was willing to admit that his son's success was due to Helena's care.

Since our Shanghai friends had moved away from Montreal we were making new friends among the people who had settled on Ridgevale Avenue. One day I went to pick up my mail and met a Czech woman named Klara Zimmer. She told me that she was from Kroměříž, a town in Moravia, where her family had a restaurant. Her father had been killed in World War I, but all the rest of the family had worked together to keep and operate the restaurant. All in all, Klara had had a happy childhood. She met her first husband at sixteen and he was the love of her life. He was a medical student, though, and they couldn't get married until he had finished his studies – by then, unfortunately, it was the turbulent year of 1938. During that time of intense persecution, when everyone was looking for a safe haven, the young doctor had received permission to work in a hospital in Africa. His new wife, Klara, could have gone with him, but she didn't want to leave her mother. They all stayed and for that she reproached herself until the end of her days. The young couple, along with Klara's mother, were deported to Theresienstadt in 1942.

Klara told me some of her unforgettable memories from there, including the story of the Berlin transports. She was put in charge of accommodating new arrivals and in 1942 there had been some transports that were comprised of groups of elderly German Jews. They were evidently well-to do-people – they had fine manners and dressed with Old World elegance. Some of the gentlemen had walking sticks with silver handles and others were wearing fine, light gray spats over their shoes. When these people got off the train, they couldn't believe the shabby misery they saw around them. They thought that there had been a terrible mistake, insisting that they had received permission from the Führer to go to a spa in Czechoslovakia. They had paid for the most luxurious hotels and now Klara had to put them up on floorboards that had been thinly covered with straw. They were bitterly disappointed and complained and blamed the Czech Jews for mistreating them – they even blamed Klara. By morning, some of these people had died from the shock.

Klara, her husband and her mother had been put on one of the infamous eastbound transports from Theresienstadt. As soon as they arrived in Auschwitz, her husband, whose childhood polio had left him with a slight limp, was selected for the gas chamber.[1] Klara survived her time in Auschwitz-Birkenau because she was young and had no children. Later she was included in a transport consigned to perform slave labour and sent from one concentration camp to another, working in factories. One day a supervisor hit her in the face, knocking off her glasses. With a cruel smirk, he then stepped on them. She still had to do her work on fine mechanics without her glasses – or else.

----

1   Upon arrival in Auschwitz and many other concentration camps, deportees were put through a selection process in which most Jews – and all mothers with children, children, elderly people and those with any disability or illness – were sent to be killed and a small number of young, physically strong prisoners were used as slave labour.

Klara had met her second husband, Pepik Zimmer, after the war and they had one daughter, Jana. We were neighbours on Ridgevale for some time, but then they bought a small house in Town of Mount Royal, an upper-income Anglophone community north of downtown Montreal. They were well established, but Pepik found the severe Montreal winters hard to bear. After ten years here, they moved to California. Despite the distance between us, I kept in touch with Klara for the rest of her life. We spoke on the telephone at least twice a week and I visited her often. She was almost blind by the time she died in San Diego in 1998.

Shortly after we moved onto Ridgevale Avenue, Milan – who was now fourteen years old – brought home a man who told me that Milan had applied to distribute the daily paper, the *Montreal Star*. Milan would earn three dollars for each route, but I had to give my consent. I told the man indignantly that children shouldn't work, but he assured me that children did these jobs in Canada. I reluctantly gave my permission. Milan wasn't content with one route, though, and I soon found out that he had taken two! He got up at five o'clock in the morning and proudly put six dollars on the kitchen table every Saturday. It was a big help. In those days I could manage with five dollars a week for groceries for one person, so Milan was practically earning his own living. The only problem that came of this was that Milan got bad bronchitis from delivering papers so early in the morning during the winter. The first time we applied for our immigration papers we were refused because of a problem with the medical examination – Milan's lungs weren't clear when he went in for his assessment. After he recovered, however, there was no problem.

In addition to school and his paper routes, Milan spent his Sundays in Côte-des-Neiges Park playing and coaching soccer – a popular sport in Europe but hardly known in Canada at the time. For doing this, he earned $1.50 for an afternoon. Milan was very keen on sports – in the fall he played football and in the winter, hockey. He was also doing very well academically, but one day, when he was in Grade 9, he came home and told me that he had quit school. I was appalled! He tried to calm me down by saying, "Mother, I promise you that I will graduate, but I just can't stand by and watch you and Daddy struggling."

Arnold had opened a jewellery store downtown, next door to Ogilvy's department store, and business was not going well. He had to compete with the local traditional jewellers like Henry Birks and Sons – if a box didn't have the Birks' name on it, the gift wasn't considered good enough, even if the value of the contents was equal or better. And at the same time, I was expecting another baby. Arnold thought that we ought to have at least one more child while we were still young. Our financial circumstances were less than auspicious, but we couldn't wait long – our biological clock was ticking. Milan was adamant that he wanted to help out and as he had promised, he kept with his schooling, attending night school at Sir George Williams College. He did so well that within eighteen months he graduated with a high school diploma. He worked during the day in the office of the CN railway station, but after he graduated, he joined the Canadian air force. He stayed in the air force for ten years while also studying for a bachelor of arts degree at Sir George and left as a captain. How he ever managed to do all of that is still a mystery to me.

～

Michael was born on October 12, 1949. We were so happy to have him join our family – my only regret was that we couldn't afford to give him the same luxuries that we had been able to give the first two children when they were born. I kept thinking about Milan's childhood, about him having a room full of toys. He even had a pedal car at ten months, way before he was old enough to use it. Michael had only thread spools to play with.

He had plenty of those because I started sewing to augment our income. I had never even held a needle in my hand before. All I knew about sewing was what I had learned from watching the dressmaker in the old days before I was married. For years, she came to the house two days a week to work on my trousseau and to make alterations to our dresses. Now, in a time of need, I made use of this little bit of skill. I typed up some business cards and distributed them around the neighbourhood. I started by adjusting the length of skirts and doing all kinds of other small alterations. Soon my little business was doing so well that, most of the time, I was able to pay the rent from my earnings.

In addition to being a dressmaker and taking care of the household, I also started offering help to sick and elderly Czech women who didn't have any family in Montreal. The first was Eva Ehrman. For a few weeks, while her husband, George, was in the hospital, I gave her a bath every day at six o'clock in the evening. I also shopped and cooked for Kitty Klein – she was thirty-five but was very ill and died after a few months. I cared for Eliska Fischel for two good years and Ada Fiala for the nine months she was in the Montreal General Hospital – every other day, I cooked her Czech meals; on the other days my friend Gerta Kadlec did the cooking. I only took care of Hedda Marle-Schiller, who was sixty-five, for a few weeks before she passed away. I had to arrange her funeral because her brother lived in Israel. Bozena Vlcek was the last woman I took care of. I cooked for her and admitted her to St. Mary's Hospital.

Despite our modest means, Michael was a beautiful, happy baby even though, as a tiny infant of only seven weeks, he had to have a hernia operation. He recovered well, though, and from then on he was a sheer delight. We bought him a playpen and he soon learned to walk around the perimeter. Unfortunately, he was in the playpen until he was almost three years old – I didn't want to let him walk freely around the apartment, in part because we had a gas stove and he liked to play with the buttons and knobs.

Michael was never bored. I talked to him while I sewed and he pretended to do his part, so that we had whole conversations before he learned to pronounce any actual words. When he was two years old, I found a nursery school on Côte-Sainte-Catherine. Arnold would take him there in the morning and I would pick him up at noon. His cousin Helenka, who was four, went to the same nursery, so right from the beginning, he always had at least one familiar face around him. He learned very fast. After he had been in the nursery for only a week, the teacher told me, "Your son already speaks English." He had apparently told her, "Mrs. Stuart, I love you!" I couldn't believe it! I had put him into the school so that he could play with other children and up until then he only spoke Czech – that was his first English sentence. He was always full of love.

In 1952 we moved from Ridgevale Avenue to a nice apartment on Décarie Boulevard. Michael was still in the nursery on Côte-Sainte-Catherine, Vera was in high school and Milan was in officer's school in Winnipeg. Arnold finally closed the jewellery store, which had lost a lot of money. Now we had to start a new business. Mr. Pachl's father owned the RUPA chocolate firm in Czechoslovakia, which had over 220 stores all over the country. His son was now in Canada, importing fine chocolates in partnership with my brother Erna, and their business was going very well. Faced with having to begin all over again from square one, Arnold decided to start a company, which he called ARVO, to sell fine chocolates to retail stores.

By this time, Michael was ready to start Grade 1. His first school was in Hampstead, on the corner of MacDonald and Dupuis, a short walk from Décarie, then just a busy crossroad. We technically belonged to the Côte-des-Neiges school district, but the school was willing to make an exception. We had Czech neighbours and their older children also went to the same school – Michael walked to school with them for two years. When he was about to enter Grade 3, in September 1957, we were told that since we belonged to another district, Michael would have to go to Iona School on Circle Road. That wasn't so far either, close enough for an eight-year-old boy to walk to by himself. His grades were mostly As, but he got an F in handwriting once. I went to see the teacher and asked her what could be done. She said, "Don't worry, he'll have three secretaries one day. He's ambitious and the F will make him work a little harder."

On October 25, 1957, Milan became a full-fledged air force officer. Arnold and I were horrified about his joining the air force, but we couldn't do anything about it. We couldn't afford to go to his graduation in Winnipeg, but he wrote to us and told us not to worry about it, that he would be returning to Montreal that same day. Unfortunately, on the day of Milan's graduation, just as our new business was beginning to pick up, our children were becoming more independent, and our lives started to seem a little easier, a sudden and unexpected disaster struck.

That day, at five o'clock in the afternoon, I received a phone call from our physician Dr. Kraft while I was at home ironing, asking me to come to his office right away, and telling me that my husband was there. Suspecting nothing, and pleasantly surprised, I exclaimed, "Oh, he came early!" We had an appointment that same evening to get polio shots and were to meet Liza and Franta there. Inoculation against polio was new in Canada, although Jonas Salk's vaccine had been available in the United States from 1955 on. To my horror, Dr. Kraft wasn't calling about the vaccines –he told me that Arnold had had a "slight" heart attack. Frantic, I dropped everything. What was I going to do with Michael? It didn't even occur to me to take him with me. It's true that I was distraught, but to this day I still regret having decided to leave him with neighbours whom I hardly knew. I later called Liza to pick him up.

When I got to Dr. Kraft's office, I found that Arnold's heart attack had not been at all "slight" – he had experienced a very serious coronary thrombosis. They took him to the intensive care unit at the Jewish General Hospital and I only found out later that the doctors had not expected him to live through the night. While he was in the hospital, everything was up to me – the family, the business, our livelihood, it was all up to me. There was no choice. Three days after Arnold's heart attack, on Monday, October 28, I took over the business. Since I was now working full-time, Michael had to stay with Liza in Ville Saint-Laurent during the day, even though my sister already had her hands full with three children of her own. Helenka was ten and the twins, Kaca and Tomy, were three.

When Arnold had recovered enough to come home after a very long and difficult six weeks, he wasn't even allowed to walk up or down stairs. That was going to be a huge problem because we lived on the third floor of a building that didn't have an elevator. I had to find a more suitable place in a hurry. It wasn't easy. Even when I managed to find something suitable, they wouldn't let me sign the lease. In the late 1950s only the head of the family – a man – could sign a lease. Three landlords refused to accept my signature. I felt helpless. "What will you do?" Liza asked me. "I'll move the furniture to the sidewalk," I replied, "call the newspapers and tell them my story! What else can I do?" "You wouldn't!" said Liza incredulously. "Oh, yes, I would," I answered with absolute determination. Convinced that I would, my sister took the matter into her own hands.

Carrying a briefcase full of twenty-dollar bills, she went to the Cummings Company office, the people who owned the building and were refusing to allow me to sign the lease. She emptied the case onto the manager's desk and suggested that the official take as much of the money as it would take to let me have whatever vacant apartment they had on the first floor. Impressed, the man accepted my signature on the lease for an apartment in a modest building in Ville Saint-Laurent. The apartment was only a temporary home – we lived there for just a few months. Soon after Arnold was released from the hospital, we started looking for a more permanent family home and in 1958 we bought a brand-new split-level house on Bois-de-Boulogne Street in the Ahuntsic district – a beautiful older section in the northern part of Montreal along the Rivière des Prairies; it was a location I had had my eye on ever since we arrived. Arnold recovered from his heart attack, but I continued to work full-time and had to do all the driving since he could no longer drive a car.

Michael finished Grade 3 in Ville Saint-Laurent and for the next school year we enrolled him in the French boarding school, L'Institut Français Évangélique. It was a co-ed school, but boys and girls had separate classes and dormitories. His cousin Helenka was there and her younger sister, Kaca, went there as well, although by that time Michael had already left. I would drive the children there on Sunday afternoons and on Friday afternoons I would bring them home for the weekend. The school, on 6600 Notre Dâme Street East, was a good hour and a half drive from where we lived. The Metropolitan Expressway, which shortened the distance, wasn't built until ten years later, for the 1967 Montreal World's Fair, Expo 67. At the beginning, this change of school must have been very hard for Michael. He was now away from home all week, in strange surroundings, among boys who spoke a language that he didn't understand. But Michael didn't complain – he knew that there was no other way.

Michael spent four years in that boarding school, finally leaving in June 1961. He was an exceptional student, well liked by his school-mates as well as by the teachers. The first year he was busy learning French, but he received a scholarship for the following three years. He remembers one very kind old nurse particularly fondly. When there was an outbreak of mumps in the school she tried to get him infected since he was young and the disease was often much worse in adults. She advised him to sleep in the same bed as boys who were already sick, but Michael must have had strong antibodies because, despite all her efforts, he never got mumps.

Vera married Jack Rubin in September 1957 and Milan married his wife, Cathy, that December. Michael was now the only child at home, and he was a great pleasure to have around.

I continued to work in the business with Arnold, who now seemed to be in surprisingly good health. On every one of our visits his cardiologist, Dr. Korenberg, would tell him, "Are you aware that your wife is keeping you alive?" We also did a wide variety of things for entertainment in those early years. In 1959 Liza's husband, Franta, built a cottage in Rawdon and we were guests there every weekend. For a few summers, we also spent time in Cape Cod with family and friends. We always had a crowd of visitors on weekends in Rawdon and since Liza wasn't the greatest cook, I became the chef. I brought cakes that I had made on Friday out to the country with me and prepared lunches and suppers there. The family was together and that's what counted.

An old Czech proverb says, "Misfortune doesn't walk over the mountain, it walks over the people." To our great sorrow, one of Liza and Franta's nine-year-old twins, Tomasek, their only son, fell ill with leukemia and from that moment on all our attention was focused on that child. Tomy died on March 30, 1962, and my poor sister's spirit died with him. It was a terrible blow for our whole family, especially for my mother – he had been her favourite grandson. Michael was devastated as well – the two boys had grown up together and Mike had lost a very good friend.

In April 1963 I had a major spine operation, the result of two slipped disks from a fall in gymnastics when I was fourteen. I had always had back pain from it but when I was about to turn fifty, I really started feeling the effects of this injury – I couldn't walk. I spent two months in the Neurological Hospital and two months in a body cast, but the operation was successful.

On May 10, 1963, my mother, Heda, died at the age of eighty-four. She had lived a hectic but mainly happy life. Our father, Max, and her children had been good to her and she to us.

From the 1960s on, Arnold and I travelled to Europe every second year – to England, Belgium, Holland, France, Switzerland, always Italy, Spain, Portugal and, naturally, Czechoslovakia. Our trip to Greece and Turkey was the most interesting.

In 1965 we got an interesting call from the URO (United Restitution Organization). A young lady by the name of Inge Callaway was inquiring about us.[2] It turned out that her grandmother's name was Wotitzky and she was a cousin of Arnold's father, Hugo Voticky. The last time I had seen Inge and her identical twin sister Renee was in Prague before the war, when they were seven or eight years old. Their mother, Erika, had been a doctor and their father a publisher. He had immigrated to Palestine alone in 1940 – he thought that "nothing could happen to women and children." We had a lot of friends who had had the same opinion, and after the war, they were all widowers.

In 1940, Erika was on her own in Prague when a proclamation was announced – not the first one and not the last one – that Jewish doctors weren't allowed to work, so she started producing face cream in her home, trying to make a living for herself and her children. In 1943, desperately trying to protect them, she cut the girls' hair, dressed them as boys, moved them to a cottage deep in the woods outside Prague and hired a woman to cook for them. After six months, without warning or explanation, Erika stopped visiting the girls and the woman lost her income. She dressed Inge and Renee as girls and took them by bus to Prague and abandoned them on the main street, Pařížská třída (Paris Road). Someone found them and called the Gestapo.

The two girls – now fifteen years old – were sent to Theresienstadt and after they had been there for one night, they were taken by train to Auschwitz. The next day, they were called to the camp gate where a car was waiting for them. Next to it stood an SS officer – Dr. Mengele – infamous for his experiments on twins.[3] He told the girls to get into

---

2   The United Restitution Organization was founded in 1948 as a legal aid society to help people living outside Germany to claim reparation and compensation for losses incurred at the hands of the Nazi regime.

3   Appointed SS garrison physician of Auschwitz in 1943, Dr. Josef Mengele was responsible for deciding which prisoners were fit for slave labour and which were to be immediately sent to the gas chambers; he conducted sadistic experiments on twins and Jewish and Roma prisoners.

the car with him and they drove to the camp hospital, where they found their mother, who was working as a doctor. Erika told the girls that she had been arrested in Prague selling her product – one of her customers turned out to be a German from Hamburg. Dr. Mengele ordered white aprons and bonnets for the sisters and told them to work as nurses. He never used Inge and Renee for experiments. The three of them were in Auschwitz from 1944 until the end of the war, when they travelled first to Prague and then to Palestine – the girls' father had immigrated to Palestine in 1940. A year after they went to Israel, Erika committed suicide. The girls both stayed in Israel and got married. Renee still lives there and Inge now lives in Montreal.

Michael graduated with a bachelor of commerce degree from McGill University in 1971 and got a job as an assistant manager at the Bank of Montreal. He quit after one year, however, and started his own advertising business. That same year he married Elizabeth, a very bright girl, but the marriage didn't last – Elizabeth didn't want to have children. Miki soon found Nancy, though, and they married in 1977. They have four beautiful, intelligent daughters – Allison, Candy, Gilly and Ashley.

Milan and his wife, Cathy, had two daughters, Linda and Liza, and Vera and Jack had two sons, Howard and Neil.

Unfortunately my husband didn't live to see the happy family. Arnold passed away on November 3, 1973, and I miss him terribly every day. I have never adjusted to being without him. I never stop crying.

Epilogue

In 1974 I moved to a one-bedroom apartment and started to work as a volunteer, first in St. Mary's Hospital and later as a cashier and book-keeper in Cummings House, the Jewish Community Centre, where I volunteered for twenty-one years, five days a week. During the winter I visited my friend Klara Zimmer in San Diego and travelled up to Santa Barbara to visit Stella Hervy. They had both lived in Montreal before moving to California.

I also started taking bridge lessons from an old Czech woman, Mrs. Skutecky, who was over eighty years old. After six private lessons she said, "Now you go among the people and play; you will make it." She was right. Bridge has helped me to keep going all these years. I used to play every day. One by one my bridge partners have all passed away, though, and now that I'm in my nineties, I have much younger partners.

The Holocaust Memorial Centre was founded in Cummings House on Côte-Sainte-Catherine in 1976 and then, in 1979, a very modest Holocaust museum opened in the basement. The first direc-tor, Krisha Starker, told me in 1982 that there would be weekly meet-ings for survivors, so I joined the club. During one of these meetings, a McGill professor, Yehudi Lindeman, told us about a program called Living Testimony and I was the only one he chose to go for an inter-view. On the first day, he asked me questions for more than an hour.

On the second day, a woman named Renata Zajdman continued. In 1994, I gave two hours of testimony in the Holocaust museum that was recorded by Gerry Singer. It was very successful. I did a third interview session in my apartment with three people sent by film-maker Steven Spielberg, but it was much less successful because the interviewer wasn't very experienced.[1]

Milan and his family, Cathy, Linda, and Liza, moved to Toronto in 1979. Michael and his family moved to Austin, Texas in 1993 – mainly because of the ongoing debate over Quebec sovereignty. On August 20, 1996, there was a demonstration in front of the Jewish General Hospital because a French-Canadian journalist had complained that the nurses had spoken English to him. I was there when some of the demonstrators gave the right-armed "Heil Hitler" salute. I jumped at them and scratched their faces and arms. I had never expected to see such people in Canada. This was apparently big news in the newspaper and on television. Michael had calls from friends in Montreal, telling him that the Voticky name was all over the newspapers.

In the late 1990s Milan started telling me that I should move to Toronto. I refused because I have some new friends in Montreal and I know the city. In 2003, Michael decided that I had to move to a retirement residence, the Waldorf. So here I am. I go out every day, and three to four times a week I play duplicate bridge in clubs. I shop for food for a few ladies who are unable to leave the building. So the time goes by.

An Austrian cameraman used Arnold's film footage from Shanghai for a documentary movie, *The Port of Last Resort*, and on March 29, 2001, the Israeli embassy in Beijing showed the film for diplomats, journalists and academics. It was a great success. Since then I've been invited to synagogues and schools – Shaare Zion Synagogue, Temple

---

1   For information on Living Testimony and Survivors of the Shoah Visual History Foundation, see the glossary.

Emanu-El, Vanier College, McGill University and Cinéma du Parc –
to talk about my experience of living through the Holocaust. In these
talks, I have thanked both the Chinese and Japanese people for saving
over 18,000 Jewish lives. On June 10, 2003, I saw a documentary on
the story of the Japanese vice consul, Mr. Sugihara, who saved over
6,000 Jewish people by giving them transit visas. Included among
these 6,000 were my parents and my sister, Liza. The last of these
events that I attended was in October 2005 in Shaar Hashomayim
Synagogue, where the majority of the 170 people invited were university and college students. Sitting next to me was a McGill student
from Hong Kong named Teresa Ho, and I'm lucky that we continue
to be in touch.

My most beloved sister, Liza, died in January 2004 after a very
long illness. In December 2005, her husband, Franta, moved to
Toronto to be with his daughter Helen. Now I only have one grandson in Montreal, Vera's son Howard, with his wife, Irene, and my two
wonderful great-grandchildren, Joshua and Daniel.

On May 28, 2006, when the Japanese Chorus was in Montreal
performing at the Temple Emanu-El, I went to see the singers at
lunch because I don't go out in the evenings anymore. I thanked them
for saving 18,000 Jews in the Shanghai ghetto. I didn't know that my
remarks had been taped, but four weeks later the Holocaust Museum
in Japan sent me the film that also included the concert. I showed
the tape at the Waldorf on August 20, 2006, and it was very well received. A few tenants even asked me if they could buy a copy. Lots of
people have told me that they have never heard of a story like mine.
I think everybody, young and old, should know what happened to us
in Europe between 1933 and 1945.

I lost so many in my family – those who weren't killed scattered
to various parts of the world. My mother's brother, my uncle Richard,
emigrated to England in 1939 with his wife, Lonca, and his son,
Honza, who was in the British air force during the war. I lost touch
with them. Richard's daughter, Hanicka, now lives somewhere in the

United States. Leo and Erik, the two sons of my mother's brother Hugo, survived the camp at Theresienstadt with their mother, Kate.

Otto Kohn's daughter, Zdenka, had gone to Palestine as a pioneer in 1924. From there she was sent to America and got a PhD in agriculture. When she returned to Israel, she became very successful in her field and she still lives there. In March 2004 she celebrated her one-hundredth birthday. I call her regularly, but I cannot visit her anymore and she cannot visit me. Her sister, Irma, died in Israel. I didn't know their whereabouts until later, when Zdenka's son, Michael, found my name in Yad Vashem when he was working on our family tree. I sent them the names of all our relatives, including those who lost their lives in the Holocaust. Like his mother, Michael also has a PhD in agriculture.

My uncle Ludvik Kohn, his wife, Hermina, and their two sons, Karel and Jirka, all perished. Ludvik committed suicide in Prague by throwing himself under the train that was taking his family to a concentration camp.

Some people ask me what helped me survive the Holocaust. In my case, it was my husband's wisdom and strength to live, as well as the fact that he supported and saved my entire family. How did I adjust to normal life? I didn't. We were in shock after the war. When we returned to Prague in 1946 there was terrible antisemitism – much more than we had ever experienced before the war. Our family had always been upright citizens and very patriotic.

My message to young people is that your whole lives should be built on honesty and loyalty to family and friends. When you choose a partner as an adult, try to give and not to expect to receive. Give to other people too and take care of the sick and the old. I did it all my life and now in my old age I get back a lot from friends and family. I believe in it.

Glossary

American Jewish Joint Distribution Committee (JDC) Also known colloquially as the "Joint." A charitable organization that provided material support for persecuted Jews in Germany and other Nazi-occupied territories and facilitated their emigration to neutral countries such as Portugal, Turkey and China. As Nazi persecution accelerated in Germany and Austria between 1933 and 1939, the JDC increased its aid to German and Austrian Jews and helped 250,000 of them escape the country, helping to cover travel expenses and landing fees, and securing travel accommodations and visas for countries of refuge. Initially operating out of Paris, when the German armies advanced toward the city in May 1940 the organization moved its offices to Lisbon, Portugal, where it continued to help thousands of European Jews find permanent refuge in the United States, Palestine and Latin America. Between 1939 and 1944, JDC officials helped close to 81,000 European Jews find asylum in various parts of the world.

Anschluss (German; literally "connection") The de facto annexation of Austria into Greater Germany by the Nazi regime in 1938. After the assassination of Austrian chancellor Engelbert Dollfuss in July 1934, Dollfuss's successor, Kurt Schuschnigg, rounded up Austrian Nazis and Social Democrats and banned opposition parties in an attempt to resist political union with Germany. Hitler met with

Schuschnigg on February 12, 1938, and demanded that he lift the ban on political parties, reinstate full party freedoms and release all imprisoned members of the Nazi party. Instead, Schuschnigg announced a plebiscite on the question of Austrian annexation (*Anschluss*), but was subsequently pressured into cancelling the plebiscite and forced to resign. When President Wilhelm Miklas refused to appoint Austrian Nazi leader Arthur Seyss-Inquart to replace Schuschnigg, Germany invaded Austria on March 12, 1938. The enthusiastic reception his forces received from the Austrian population gave Hitler the cover to annex Austria outright on March 13. The German army marched in to solidify the annexation and a Nazi-controlled plebiscite held under strict Nazi supervision on April 10 were 99.7 per cent in favour of the *Anschluss*. Austria was renamed Õstmark and ceased to exist as a separate nation until 1945.

Auschwitz (German name for the Polish town Oświęcim) A town in southern Poland approximately thirty-seven kilometres from Krakow and the name of the largest complex of concentration camps built nearby. The Auschwitz complex contained three main camps: Auschwitz I, established in May 1940 mainly to hold Polish prisoners; Auschwitz II-Birkenau, a mass-murder facility built in 1942; and Auschwitz III-Monowitz, a slave-labour camp built in October 1942. In 1941, Auschwitz I was the testing site for the use of the lethal gas Zyklon B as a method of mass killing. The Auschwitz complex was liberated by the Soviet army in January 1945.

blood libel The false accusation that Jews use the blood of Christian children to prepare the matzah for Passover. It is one of the most persistent forms of antisemitism in Europe, dating back to the thirteenth century. *See also* matzah and Passover.

Bohemian Forest (Böhmerwald, German; in Czech, Šumava) A 120-kilometre-long low mountain range that forms a natural border between what is now the Czech Republic on one side and Germany and Austria on the other. Šumava is also used in Czech as the name for the entire surrounding region on the Czech side of the mountains.

cantor (Hebrew: *chazzan*) A person who leads a Jewish congregation in prayer. Because music plays such a large role in Jewish religious services, the cantor is usually professionally trained in music.

Charles I (Charles Francis Joseph Louis Hubert George Mary of Habsburg-Lorraine) The successor to Franz Josef I, Charles I (1887–1922) of Austria, who was also Charles IV of Hungary, was the last ruler of the Austro-Hungarian Empire from 1916 to 1918, and was also the last emperor of Austria as well as the last king of Hungary, Bohemia, Croatia, and Galicia and Lodomeria (now Poland and Ukraine).

Churchill, Winston (1874–1965) A British statesman who was prime minister of the United Kingdom from 1940 to 1945, and again from 1951 to 1955. A fierce opponent of Nazism from its inception, Churchill led his country in the fight against Nazi Germany and became a key member of the Allied leadership of both the war effort and the post-war peace settlement.

Dachau The Nazis' first concentration camp, which was established primarily to house political prisoners in March 1933. The Dachau camp was located about sixteen kilometres northwest of Munich in southern Germany. The number of Jews interned there rose considerably after Kristallnacht on November 10, 1938. In 1942 a crematorium area was constructed next to the main camp. By the spring of 1945, Dachau and its subcamps held more than 67,665 registered prisoners – 43,350 categorized as political prisoners, and 22,100 as Jews. As the American Allied forces neared the camp in April 1945, the Nazis forced 7,000 prisoners, primarily Jews, on a gruelling death march to Tegernsee, another camp in southern Germany.

fifth column A term first used by the Nationalists in the Spanish Civil War of 1936–1939 to refer to their supporters within the territories controlled by the Republican side. Because these people were helping the four columns of the Nationalists' army, they were deemed to be their "fifth column." Since that time the expression has been used to designate a group of people who are clandestinely collaborating with an invading enemy.

French Concession An area located in the northwestern part of Shanghai that was conceded to the French by the Chinese in 1849, after the Chinese surrendered the city as a condition of the Treaty of Nanking that concluded the First Opium War between Britain and China. A concession is a territory within another country that is administered by an entity different than the state that is sovereign – territory that is "conceded" by the weaker power to the stronger power. After 1849, Shanghai was opened up to unrestricted foreign trade and the British, French and Americans each took possession and control of a designated area of the city.

Geneva Conventions A set of treaties and protocols that were negotiated over the period 1864–1949 to establish an international law for the standards of humanitarian treatment of victims of war, both military and civilian.

German Rearmament Nazi Germany's 1935 program of rearmament in contravention of the terms of the 1919 Treaty of Versailles that ended World War I. Announced in March 1935 by Joseph Goebbels, Nazi Minister for Popular Enlightenment and Propaganda, Germany proceeded to establish an air force and greatly increased the size of its army. Although Italy, France and Belgium protested these actions, they did nothing to curtail them. On June 18, 1935, Britain signed the Anglo-German naval agreement that allowed Germany to maintain a navy that was one-third the size of the British fleet. Hitler renounced the agreement on April 28, 1939.

Gestapo (German) Short for Geheime Staatspolizei, the Secret State Police of Nazi Germany. The Gestapo were a brutal force that operated with very few legal constraints in dealing with the perceived enemies of the Nazi regime and were responsible for rounding up European Jews for deportation to the death camps.

They were also responsible for issuing exit visas to the residents of German-occupied areas. A number of Gestapo members also joined the Einsatzgruppen, the mobile killing squads responsible for the roundup and murder of Jews in eastern Poland and the USSR through mass shooting operations.

Goebbels, Joseph (1897–1945) One of Hitler's closest associates and zealous followers. Goebbels was appointed Nazi Minister for Popular Enlightenment and Propaganda on March 13, 1933, and given the mandate of "Nazifying" Germany. To this end, he began with book burnings and soon established total state control over media, the arts and information. He is also known for having perfected the "Big Lie" propaganda technique – based on the principle that if an audacious lie is asserted and repeated enough times, it will be generally believed. A virulent antisemite, Goebbels initiated the Nazis' organized attacks against German Jews, beginning with boycotts and culminating in Kristallnacht, the violent pogrom against German Jews in November 1938. He remained with Hitler to the end; he and his wife killed their six young children and then committed suicide.

Gymnasium (German) A word used throughout central and eastern Europe to mean high school.

Hagibor swim team The renowned pre–World War II Jewish swim team from the Hagibor Jewish sports club in Prague.

Hongkew (Hongkou) The district of Shanghai located north and east of the Suzhou River that was settled by American colonists in 1848, when it was known as the American Concession (signifying that it was controlled and governed by the United States, though China maintained nominal sovereignty). In 1863, when the Americans and British held joint control over the area, it became known as the International Settlement. In 1943, the Jewish ghetto was established in Hongkew; at this time it was poor, dilapidated and extremely overcrowded.

Italo-Abyssinian War (October 1935–May 1936) The war between Italy and Ethiopia that was fought for control over the Horn of Africa and that resulted in Italy's occupation of Ethiopia. During the war, Italian military commanders used air power and poison gas to separate and destroy Ethiopian emperor Haile Selassie's poorly equipped armies. Also referred to as the Second Italo-Ethiopian War.

Japan-China War (1937–1945) The eight-year conflict that resulted from Japan's attempt to occupy and control China. During the war, various regions were decimated and more than twenty million people were killed. Also referred to as the second Sino-Japanese war.

Jewish Brigade A battalion that was formed in September 1944 under the command of the British Eighth Army. The Jewish Brigade included more than 5,000 volunteers from Palestine. After the war, the Brigade was essential in helping refugees and organizing their entry into Palestine. It was disbanded by the British in mid-1946.

Josef, Franz (1830–1916) Ruler of the Austro-Hungarian Empire from 1848–1916.

Kindertransport (German; literally "children's transport") The organized attempts by British and American groups to get Jewish children out of Nazi Germany before 1939. Between December 1938 and September 1939, the government-sanctioned but privately funded Kindertransport rescued nearly 10,000 children under the age of seventeen. There were also 1,400 children under the age of fourteen who went to the US between 1934 and 1945, through a program known as "One Thousand Children," which was initiated and run by private and communal organizations. Individual Jewish religious schools in both the UK and the US also offered rabbinical training to German Jewish youths so that they would qualify for exit visas before 1939. A February 1939 US government initiative to admit 20,000 Jewish child refugees from Nazi Germany to the United States failed to get Congressional support.

kosher (Hebrew) Fit to eat according to Jewish dietary laws. Observant Jews follow a system of rules known as kashruth that regulates what can be eaten, how food is prepared and how meat and
poultry are slaughtered. Food is kosher when it has been deemed
fit for consumption according to this system of rules. There are
several foods that are forbidden, most notably pork products and
shellfish.

Kristallnacht (German; literally "Night of Broken Glass") A series
of pogroms that took place in Germany and Austria on November 9–10, 1938. Over the course of twenty-four hours, ninety-one
Jews were murdered, 25,000–30,000 were arrested and deported
to concentration camps, two hundred synagogues were destroyed
and thousands of Jewish businesses and homes were ransacked.
Planned by the Nazis as a coordinated attack on the Jews of Germany and Austria, Kristallnacht is often seen as an important
turning point in Hitler's policies of systematic persecution of Jews.

Living Testimony A Holocaust research and documentation project started at McGill University in Montreal in 1989 by Professor
Emeritus Yehudi Lindeman.

mahjong A four-player game that uses tiles as playing pieces and
originated in China.

Masaryk, Jan (1866–1948) A liberal-democratic politician who was
the son of Tomas G. Masaryk, first president of Czechoslovakia.
He served as foreign minister to the Czech government-in-exile
during World War II, a position he retained in the provisional,
multi-party National Front government in 1945. In 1948, after the
consolidation of a Communist, Soviet-led government, Masaryk
was found dead in his pyjamas in the courtyard of his apartment
building. There was ongoing debate and investigations into whether he committed suicide, as was proclaimed by the Communist
government, or whether he was thrown to his death by Communist thugs. The final investigation in 2002, which was concluded
in December 2003, proved that Masaryk was murdered through

the testimony of an expert witness who studied the position of the body when it was found. However, this new evidence did not lead to any prosecutions.

Masaryk, Tomáš G. (1850–1937) The founder and first president of Czechoslovakia. He was known for his strong public opposition to antisemitism.

matzah (Hebrew, also matza, matzoh, matsah; in Yiddish, matze) Crisp flatbread made of white plain flour and water that is not allowed to rise before or during baking. Matzah is the substitute for bread during the Jewish holiday of Passover, when eating bread and leavened products is forbidden. *See also* Passover.

Mauthausen A notoriously brutal Nazi concentration camp that was located about twenty kilometres east of the Austrian city of Linz. Mauthausen was first established shortly after the annexation of Austria to imprison "asocial" political opponents of the Third Reich. By the end of the war, close to 200,000 prisoners had passed through the Mauthausen forced-labour camp system and almost 120,000 of them died there – including 38,120 Jews – from starvation, disease and hard labour. The US army liberated the camp on May 5, 1945.

Meisinger, Josef (1899–1947) The chief Gestapo representative to Japan. Colonel Josef Meisinger arrived in Shanghai in July 1942 with instructions to carry out the "Final Solution against the Jews" there. Before arriving in Shanghai, Meisinger had been Gestapo chief in Poland, where his violence earned him the nickname the "Brutal Butcher of Warsaw."

Mengele, Dr. Josef (1911–1979) The SS garrison physician of Auschwitz from May 1943 to January 1945. Dr. Josef Mengele was responsible for deciding which prisoners were fit for slave labour and which were to be immediately sent to the gas chambers; he often conducted sadistic experiments on twins and Jewish and Roma prisoners.

Munich Pact An agreement signed in the early hours of September 30, 1938, by Nazi Germany, France, Britain and Italy. The Munich Pact gave Nazi Germany permission to annex the strategically important Sudeten region of Czechoslovakia in a failed attempt to appease Hitler and prevent war. Czechoslovakia was not invited to participate in the crucial conference in Munich that would determine its fate. *See also* Sudetenland crisis.

Nuremberg Laws The September 1935 laws that stripped Jews of their civil rights as German citizens and separated them from Germans legally, socially and politically. They were first announced at the Nazi party rally in the city of Nuremberg in 1933. Under "The Law for the Protection of German Blood and Honor" Jews were defined as a separate race rather than a religious group; whether a person was racially Jewish was determined by ancestry (how many Jewish grandparents a person had). Among other things, the laws forbade marriages or sexual relations between Jews and Germans.

Passover (in Hebrew, Pesach) One of the major festivals of the Jewish calendar. Passover commemorates the liberation and exodus of the Israelite slaves from Egypt during the reign of the Pharaoh Ramses II. Occurring in the spring, the festival lasts for eight days and begins with a lavish ritual meal called a seder during which the story of Exodus is retold through the reading of a Jewish religious text called the Haggadah. With its special foods, songs and customs, the seder is the focal point of the Passover celebration and is traditionally a time of family gathering. During Passover Jews refrain from eating *chametz* – that is, anything that contains barley, wheat, rye, oats, and spelt that has undergone fermentation as a result of contact with liquid. The name of the festival refers to the fact that God "passed over" the houses of the Jews when He set about slaying the firstborn sons of Egypt as the last of the ten plagues aimed at convincing Pharaoh to free the Jews.

Pearl Harbor A US naval base at Pearl Harbor on Oahu Island, Hawaii. Pearl Harbor usually refers to the December 7, 1941, surprise aerial attack on the base by Japanese forces. It is the event that led to the entrance of the US as a combatant in World War II. The background to the attack was a deterioration in relations between the United States and Japan throughout the 1930s, which had come to a head over three significant events: Japan's invasion of China in 1937, the country's alliance with Germany and Italy in 1940 and Japan's occupation of French Indochina on July 1941. Later that month, the US froze Japanese assets in the US and declared an embargo on shipments of petroleum and other vital war materials to Japan. By late 1941, the US had severed almost all commercial and financial relations with Japan. Japan continued to negotiate with the US, but, in the meantime, the Japanese government was preparing for war and eventually attacked on December 7.

poste restante (French; literally "post that remains") A postal service that allows the recipient of the mail to come and pick it up at the post office, as opposed to having the letter directly delivered to their residence; often called general delivery mail.

Protectorate of Bohemia and Moravia (German: Protektorat Böhmen und Mähren; Czech: Protektorát Čechy a Morava) The name given by the Nazis to the majority ethnic-Czech regions of Bohemia, Moravia and Czech Silesia that they invaded and occupied on March 15, 1939. These areas now make up the present-day Czech Republic.

Ravensbrück The largest Nazi concentration camp designed almost exclusively for women. Located about ninety kilometres north of Berlin, it first opened in May 1939 under the direction of SS leader Heinrich Himmler. Various subcamps were built in the area around Ravensbrück throughout the war to serve as forced labour camps. From 1942 on, the complex served as one of the main training facilities for female SS guards. Medical experiments were also carried out on the women at Ravensbrück and in early 1945 the SS built a gas chamber, where approximately 5,000 to 6,000 prisoners were gassed. More than 100,000 women prisoners from all over Nazi-occupied Europe had passed through Ravensbrück before the Soviets liberated the camp on April 29-30, 1945; about 3 per cent of the camp population was Czech. It is estimated that some 50,000 women died in the camp.

Rhineland Crisis of 1936 (German: Rheinland; French: Rhénanie) A crisis that was sparked on March 7, 1936, when Hitler repudiated the Rhineland clauses of the 1919 Treaty of Versailles, as well as the 1925 non-aggression pact between France, Germany, Britain, Italy and Belgium known as the Locarno Treaty, and German troops entered the demilitarized zone. The historically controversial area is located in western Germany and lies along both banks of the middle Rhine River, on the eastern side of Germany's border with France, Luxembourg, Belgium and the Netherlands. Unaware that Hitler had instructed his troops to retreat if the French invaded, the French general staff refused to act unless partial mobilization was ordered, which the French Cabinet refused. The French Cabinet also concluded that it should do nothing without the full agreement of the British, who declined to respond to the German challenge.

Rosh Hashanah (Hebrew) New Year. The autumn holiday that marks the beginning of the Jewish year and ushers in the High Holy Days. It is observed by a synagogue service that ends with blowing the *shofar* (horn), which marks the beginning of the holiday. The service is usually followed by a family dinner where traditional and symbolic foods are eaten. *See also* Yom Kippur.

Russo-Japanese War (1904–1905) The war between Russia and Japan that was fought over territory in Manchuria and Korea.

SA The abbreviation for Sturmabteilung (German) or "assault division," but usually translated as "storm troopers." The SA served as the paramilitary wing of the Nazi party and played a key role in Hitler's rise to power in the 1930s. Members of the SA were often called "Brown Shirts" for the colour of their uniforms, which distinguished them from Heinrich Himmler's all-black SS (Schutzstaffel) uniforms. The SA was effectively superseded by the SS after the 1934 purge within the Nazi party known as the "Night of the Long Knives."

Schiff, Jacob Henry (1847–1920) One of the leading railroad bankers in the United States. Schiff played a key role in securing $200 million in loans for the Japanese during the 1904–1905 Russo-Japanese War. He was subsequently decorated by the emperor of Japan.

shiva (Hebrew; literally: seven) In Judaism, the seven-day mourning period that is observed after the funeral of a close family relation.

Spanish Civil War (1936–1939) The war in Spain between the military – supported by Conservative, Catholic and fascist elements – and the Republican government. Sparked by an initial coup that failed to win a decisive victory, the country was plunged into a bloody civil war. It ended when the Nationalists, under the leadership of General Francisco Franco, marched into Madrid. During the civil war, the Nationalists received aid from both Fascist Italy and Nazi Germany, and the Republicans received aid from volunteers worldwide.

SS Abbreviation for Schutzstaffel (Defence Corps). The SS was established in 1925 as Adolf Hitler's elite corps of personal bodyguards. Under the directorship of its leader, Heinrich Himmler, its membership grew from 280 in 1929 to 50,000 when the Nazis came to power in 1933, and to nearly a quarter of a million on the eve of World War II. The SS was comprised of the Allgemeine-SS (General SS) and the Waffen-SS (Armed, or Combat SS). The General SS dealt with policing and the enforcement of Nazi racial policies in Germany and the Nazi-occupied countries. An important unit within the SS was the Reichssicherheitshauptamt (RSHA, the Central Office of Reich Security), whose responsibility included the Gestapo (Geheime Staatspolizei). The SS ran the concentration and death camps, with all their associated economic enterprises, and also fielded its own Waffen-SS military divisions, including some recruited from the occupied countries. *See also* Gestapo.

Sudetenland crisis A crisis sparked by the Nazi demand for the "return" of the Sudetenland – the western border region of Czechoslovakia inhabited primarily by ethnic Germans – to allow the repatriation into the Third Reich of the area's ethnic German population. The major powers of Europe held a conference in Munich, Germany to negotiate the fate of the Sudetenland without the presence of Czechoslovakia. In what ended up being a failed attempt at appeasing Nazi Germany, the Munich Pact was signed by Nazi Germany, France, Britain and Italy in the early hours of September 30, 1938. The Sudeten region that was ceded to Germany was of incalculable strategic and economic importance to Czechoslovakia – it was the location of most of the country's border defenses, many of its banks, 70 per cent of its iron and steel industry and 70 per cent of its electrical power.

Sudetenland rally A Nazi Party rally held in September 1938 in the Bavarian city of Nuremberg; part of an annual propaganda event held between 1923 and 1938. The theme of the 1938 rally, which took place on September 5–12, was "Grossdeutschland" (Greater Germany). Hitler spoke of the Sudeten Germans and the "natural right of the unification of all Germans," not by negotiation but by force – that they were not defenseless and had not been abandoned. By the end of the broadcast of Hitler's closing address, many Sudeten Germans were rioting in the streets. Czechoslovak president Edvard Beneš declared martial law in the region and in response, Sudeten-German leader Konrad Henlein, acting on Hitler's directives to provoke the Czechoslovakian government, issued a six-hour ultimatum demanding an end to martial law. Instead, Beneš called in more troops and quelled the riots.

Sugihara, Chiune (1900–1986) A Japanese diplomat stationed in Lithuania in 1940 who was responsible for saving the lives of more than 6,000 Jews by issuing transit visas through Japan. Sugihara ignored orders from his superiors that required Jews to have the correct documentation in order to be issued visas, and instead issued visas to everyone who came to him. He empathized with the Jews' plight and worked tirelessly to provide the visas – often signing more than three hundred a day – until the consulate was closed at the end of August 1940. He left his official visa stamp behind in Kovno, which allowed hundreds of forged Sugihara visas to be issued as well. He was stationed briefly in Prague between September 1940 and February 1941, where he continued to issue visas to Jewish refugees. In 1985, he was awarded the title of "Righteous Among the Nations" by the Yad Vashem Martyrs' and Heroes' Remembrance Authority in Jerusalem.

Survivors of the Shoah Visual History Foundation A project founded by Steven Spielberg in 1994 as a result of his experience making the film *Schindler's List*. Its mission is to record and preserve the testimonies of Holocaust survivors in a video archive and to promote Holocaust education. In 2006, after recording almost 50,000 international testimonies, the foundation partnered with the University of Southern California and became the USC Shoah Foundation Institute for Visual History and Education.

Theresienstadt (Terezin in Czech) A walled town in the Czech Republic, sixty kilometres north of Prague, that served as both a ghetto and a concentration camp between 1941 and 1945. More than 73,000 Jews from the German Protectorate of Bohemia and Moravia and from the Greater German Reich (including Austria and parts of Poland) were deported to Terezin between November 24, 1941 and March 30, 1945, the majority of them arriving in 1942. More than 60,000 of them were deported to Auschwitz or other death camps. Terezin was showcased as a "model" ghetto for propaganda purposes to demonstrate to delegates from the International Red Cross and others the "humane" treatment of Jews and to counter information reaching the Allies about Nazi atrocities and mass murder. The ghetto was liberated on May 8, 1945, by the Soviet Red Army.

Treaty of Versailles One of the five treaties produced at the 1919 Paris Peace Conference organized by the victors of World War I. The Treaty of Versailles imposed a harsh and punitive peace on Germany, including high reparations, restrictions on German military rearmament and activities, and the redrawing of Germany's borders, resulting in the loss of territory.

Treblinka One of the camps created as part of Operation Reinhard, the Nazi plan for murdering Jews in German-occupied Poland using poison gas. A slave-labour camp (Treblinka I) was built in November 1941 in the *Generalgouvernement*, near the villages of Treblinka and Makinia Górna, about 80 kilometres northeast of Warsaw. Treblinka II, the killing centre, was constructed in a sparsely populated and heavily wooded area about 1.5 kilometres from the labour camp in 1942. The first massive from Warsaw began on July 22, 1942. The people who arrived in the deportations to Treblinka II packed into railway freight cars were separated by sex, stripped of their clothing and other possessions, marched into buildings that they were told contained bathhouses and gassed with carbon monoxide. From July 1942 to October 1943 more than 750,000 Jews were killed at Treblinka, making it second only to Auschwitz in the numbers of Jews killed. Treblinka I and II were both liberated by the Soviet army in July 1944.

United Nations Relief and Rehabilitation Administration (UNRRA) An organization created at a 44-nation conference in Washington, DC on November 9, 1943, to provide economic assistance to Nazi-occupied European nations following World War II and to repatriate and assist war refugees.

United Restitution Organization (URO) Organization founded in 1948 as a legal aid society to help people living outside Germany, with limited financial means, to claim reparation and compensation due to them for losses incurred at the hands of the Nazi regime.

Wehrmacht (German) The Germany army during the Third Reich.

Yom Kippur (Hebrew; literally "Day of Atonement") A solemn day of fasting and repentance that comes eight days after Rosh Hashanah, the Jewish New Year, and marks the end of the High Holy Days. *See also* Rosh Hashanah.

zither A stringed instrument in which the strings are stretched across a flat wooden soundbox and played horizontally with either the fingers or a pick, or plectrum. It is most commonly played in Central Europe and East Asia.

Photographs

1 Anka at about age one, 1914.

2 Anka's parents, Max and Hedvika Kanturek, 1938.

3 Anka, age seven, (left) and her sister, Liza, age three, with Fanda, the Kantureks' maid. Prague, 1920.

1 The Kanturek family. Prague, 1929. Left to right: (behind) Anka's brother, Vilda; Anka; and her brother Erna; (in front) Anka's father, Max; her mother, Hedvika; and her sister, Liza.

2 and 3 Anka, age sixteen, at two masquerade balls. Prague, 1930–1931.

1

2

1 Anka and Arnold Voticky's engagement picture. Prague, May 8, 1932.

2 Members of Arnold Voticky's family. Arnold's father, Hugo Voticky, is in front
   (second from the left); his brother Franta is in the centre of the back row; Arnold's sister-in-law, Franta's wife, Vlasta, is third from the left in the back; and
   Vlasta's brother, Pepik Kolinsky, is in the back on the far left. Prague, circa 1930.

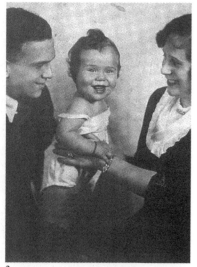

1

2

3

1 Anka (left), pregnant with her first child, Milan; with her mother-in-law, Olga
   Voticky (centre), and Arnold. Prague, 1933.

2 Arnold and Anka with baby Milan, 1934.

3 Milan with his first cousin, Harry Knopfelmacher, who was born on the same
   night. Prague, 1937.

Anka (right) and Arnold (in front) on holiday with Arnold's sister Greta (centre) and her husband, Armin Knopfelmacher (left). Spindelmühle, 1936.

1 Anka (left) with her friends Marta Mautnerova (centre) and Lidka Smolkova (right). Prague, 1936.

2 Anka on another skiing holiday in Spindelmühle, 1937.

1

2

1 Milan trying on his gas mask at age four. Prague, 1938.

2 Arnold Voticky, just before leaving for Shanghai. Prague, 1940.

1 Anka with her family on the way to Shanghai on the SS *Conte Rosso*, 1940. Left to right (behind) Arnold; Anka; her friend, Lidka Winter; Lidka's husband, Rudla; Anka's brother Erna; and his wife, Hilda; (in front): Milan; Vera; Eva Winter; and Anka's niece Eva Kanturek.

2 The children – Milan (left), Vera (centre) and Anka's niece Eva Kanturek (right) in Shanghai.

1 Czech officials at the Czech consulate in Shanghai, 1941, with Milan (far left).
   Second from the left is Czech military attaché Vladimir Taussig; the Czech Scout-
   master is second from the right; and the Czech consul, Mr. Stepan, is on the far
   right.

2 Milan with Mr. Stepan at the Czech consulate for a celebration of Tomás Masaryk's birthday. Shanghai, 1941.

1 Anka buying eggs (100 for one dollar) at the Shanghai market.

2 Liza (second from right) while she was the supervisor at Czech house in the Hongkew ghetto. Shanghai, 1943.

3 Milan in his soccer uniform. Shanghai, 1942.

4 Milan (second row, far right) with his soccer team. Erna (third row, left), was the coach. Shanghai, 1942.

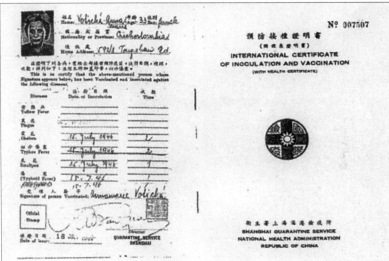

1　The Votickys in front of the house they built in the Hongkew ghetto. Left to right: Vera, Arnold, Anka and Milan. Shanghai, 1945.

2　Anka's Chinese-government-issued certificate of inoculation, 1946.

1

2

1   Anka (left) with Fanda after the war. Prague, 1947.

2   A street sign in Prague, across from the Jewish cemetery, that carries the Voticky name. The photo was taken by Anka's granddaughter in 2005.

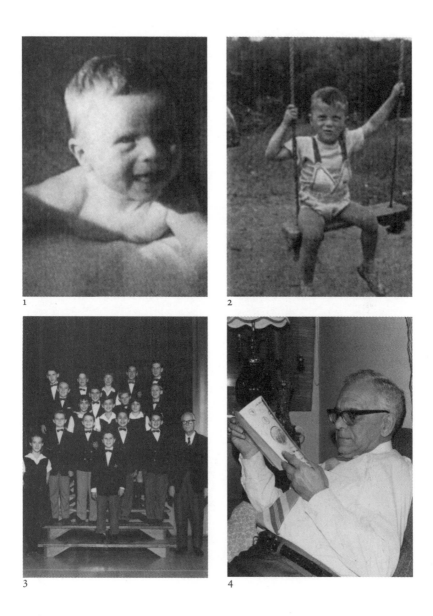

1 Anka and Arnold's third child, Michael, as a baby. Montreal, 1950.

2 Michael at about two and a half. Montreal, 1952.

3 Michael (front row centre) with his class at L'Institut Français Évangélique. Montreal, 1959.

4 Arnold Voticky. Montreal, 1972.

1 Anka with Yoshi Tamura, a member of Beit Shalom Japan, who came to Montreal with Makhelat Hashachar (Shinonome Chorus) in May 2006. In October 2006 he returned to Montreal to record Anka's testimony about her experiences in Shanghai.

2 Anka with Akira Kondo, another member of Beit Shalom Japan. Montreal, October 2006.

Index

The Azrieli Foundation was established in 1989 to realize and extend the philanthropic vision of David J. Azrieli, C.M., C.Q., M.Arch. The Foundation's mission is to support a wide spectrum of initiatives in education and research. The Azrieli Foundation is an active supporter of programs in the fields of Jewish education, the education of architects, scientific and medical research, and education in the arts. The Azrieli Foundation's many well-known initiatives include: the Holocaust Survivor Memoirs Program, which collects, preserves, publishes and distributes the written memoirs of survivors in Canada; the Azrieli Institute for Educational Empowerment, an innovative program successfully working to keep at-risk youth in school; and the Azrieli Fellows Program, which promotes academic excellence and leadership on the graduate level at Israeli universities.